FD9

5.95

HAILWOOD

Also by Mike Hailwood:

THE ART OF MOTOR CYCLE RACING
(with Murray Walker)

HAILWOOD

MIKE HAILWOOD AND TED MACAULEY

CASSELL · LONDON

CASSELL & COMPANY LTD
35 Red Lion Square, London WC1
Melbourne, Sydney, Toronto
Johannesburg, Auckland

First published 1968

S.B.N. 304 93240 x

Printed in Great Britain by
Cox and Wyman Ltd, London, Fakenham and Reading
F.768

Contents

1 1968—World Champion 1
2 Pangbourne 8
3 First Steps 19
4 TT Hat-Trick 37
5 MV 47
6 One Day's Work 55
7 Honda 76
8 The Car Game 91
9 Three to Remember 109

To Stan,
with
Gratitude
for Everything

Illustrations

Between pp. 16 and 17
How it all started (*Stan Hailwood*)
Showing he can ride horses too (*Stan Hailwood*)
The budding naval officer (*Stan Hailwood*)
It ain't much, but it's home (*Motor Cycle*)
Castle Combe, 1957
His style beginning to show
First TT (*Nick Nicholls*)

Between pp. 32 and 33
Oulton Park, 1958 (*Nick Nicholls*)
Production racing in the Thruxton 500-miler (*Motor Cycle*)
On the 250 NSU in South Africa (*A. Daulman, Port Elizabeth*)
With Dave Chadwick and Frank Cope (*Eastern Province Herald*)
Grasstracking a Matchless
With Bill Lacey at the 1958 TT
With Provini and Ubbiali

Between pp. 48 and 49
At the Ulster GP, 1959 (*Motor Cycling*)
Practice for the 1959 TT (*Nick Nicholls*)
The 250 Ducati (*Nick Nicholls*)
After the 1960 Senior
First Japanese TT Victory (*Motor Cycling*)

Between pp. 64 and 65
With Phillis and Taveri at the 1961 TT
In the winner's enclosure, 1961 (*Motor Cycling*)
First try-out on a works MV
The Scottish Six Days Trial (*Ron Osborn*)
The Ecurie Sportive workshop (*Motor Cycle*)
Polishing some of the pots (*Motor Cycle*)
Balance is the thing (*Volker Rauch, Nürnberg*)
Vittorio Carrano (*Volker Rauch*)

ILLUSTRATIONS

Between pp. 80 and 81
An all-night session at Monza (*Volker Rauch*)
Autographing at Brands Hatch (*Nicholas Flower*)
The eyes of a man of speed (*Volker Rauch*)
First car race at Brands (*E. Gerry Stream*)
With Graham Hill and Paddy Driver
A spill in East Germany (*Manfred Löscher, Zwickau*)
At the Nürburgring, 1964 (*G. L. Bramstedt*)
Planning the book at Hockenheim (*Volker Rauch*)
Five years' difference (*Volker Rauch*)

Between pp. 96 and 97
At Clermont Ferrand (*Volker Rauch*)
John Hartle at Dundrod (*Volker Rauch*)
After the TT spill on the MV
With Agostini and John Cooper at Brno (*Volker Rauch*)
Honda and MV
Discussing tactics with Jim Redman (*Volker Rauch*)
Crashing at Monza, 1962 . . . (*Corriere della Sera*)
. . . and Modena, 1964 . . . (*Coltrin, Modena*)
and Brands, 1963 (*Planet News*)

1 1968—World Champion

The name of Mike Hailwood is synonymous with independence. That is the first impression one forms when one's familiarity with him goes beyond first-name terms and develops into friendship. Before this it is easy to mistake his independence for coldness and even conceit. The truth is that he is shy and suffers from an inferiority complex.

There are many people who pretend to understand him; they imagine they know what makes him tick. There are many more who do not understand him, and who, through ignorance, because there is no text-book to tell them all about him, consider him to be self-centred and difficult. Neither the first group with its pretensions nor the second with its unwitting ignorance could ever hope to grasp the simple answer to what lies inside the man. The roots of his independence can be traced only through knowing him, and so only a handful of people are aware of its origins.

From the age of three onwards, he has lived remote from the close confines of day-to-day family life, first in nursery schools and boarding-schools, later in hotels and flats around the world. Independence breeds easily in such circumstances. More than that, it becomes an absolute necessity; and once it is established, it is a code of life.

Mike has told me that his father, Stanley, used to rule him with an iron hand. This rigidity of control, enforced in an uncompromising manner and accentuated by his living away from home, has left Mike in a position where he depends on nobody. He is more self-sufficient than anybody I know.

Stanley Hailwood, with his wisdom and energy, has been the pushing power behind the champion. He is the man who first saw the talent there was in Mike, and he did more than anyone else to foster it, shape it, and, with his boundless enthusiasm, encourage it. This factor in Mike's upbringing has largely eliminated the conventional father–son relationship and substituted in its place a long-standing friendship that probably goes deeper than any more normal parent-and-child understanding.

If Stanley had not been the sort of man he was—and is—he could easily have stifled Mike's natural talent. Fortunately this tough North Countryman, who owes his prosperity to his own spirit and hard work, has never been the sort of man to let his son coast through life, in the manner of many heirs to fortunes. Stanley had fought his own battles and had made his own life comfortable by his single-mindedness; he had built up the biggest motor-cycle sales business in the country. The pride he felt in his son did not show itself until Mike began to make his own way; then he gave all the help he could, when he considered it was most needed.

Mike selects his own company; nobody chooses him. It is one more mark of his self-reliance that the circle is exclusive and tightly knit. He says he has only six close friends in the world. Because he is a celebrity, he is wary in his readiness to accept people, wondering all the time if they want to know him merely because he is who he is. This is one of the penalties of fame, which Mike shares with all men of high achievement. It makes the defence of his privacy a hardship; his answer is to be as elusive as possible. But it does make him wonder if he would be as popular if he were plain Mike Hailwood, if he were something other than a world champion.

At the Ulster Grand Prix one year, his urge to test the qualities of Hailwood the man against those of Hailwood the champion came to a head. At our hotel in Belfast there were hundreds of people who had travelled from all over Ireland to get a glimpse of him; I knew he was bored by the ceaseless requests for autographs, and frustrated in his efforts to find some privacy outside the even greater boredom and loneliness of his bedroom. So when the phone rang in my room it was no surprise to hear Mike saying, 'Let's get out of here. I'd like to go to a dance where nobody knows me. I want to see how I get on as an ordinary bloke.'

We drove to a dance-hall, and within a few minutes Mike had slipped anonymously into the crowd; he was enjoying himself enormously. But his pleasure came to an end when a sharp-eyed compère on the stage spotted him among the dancers. He silenced the band. Then he guided the spotlight into the crowd, and onto Mike and the girl he was dancing with. Mike was furious, and left the ballroom. His experiment was no longer valid, because he assumed the girls would only dance with him because he was famous.

'That's the trouble with me, my inferiority complex,' he said as we drove back to the hotel. 'I'll never know who really wants to be friendly with me and who just wants to be seen talking to a champion. At race-meetings, for instance, I couldn't bring myself to go over and talk to a girl I didn't know. What right have I to approach a girl just because I'm the champion? I suppose they'd feel the same.'

Is it shyness? 'I suppose so,' said Mike; 'when I meet a girl for the first time I can hardly speak. I bumble along talking all sorts of rubbish.'

Outside Mike's circle of personal friends are legions of essential business contacts, whom he receives with consideration and charm but who still remain at arm's length. They are a necessary part of his public life, but there is little or no room for them when he is seeking privacy.

The trade barons, the competitions managers, are the men who annually tempt Mike with fat contracts; they steer him smoothly through the complexities of business. They know and understand his vagaries and, without exception, respect him. Derek Carpenter, Dunlop's young Competitions Manager, says, 'If everybody else was as easy to deal with as Mike, our job would be so much easier.'

Probably Mike's greatest failing is his lack of patience; but this is often sorely tried, usually by autograph- and souvenir-hunters. More than anybody else, the autograph-hunters have suffered stinging rebukes; their persistence has all too often invited it. While Mike is grateful for their anxiety to add his signature to their collection, he is mystified by their lack of understanding, their rudeness and their invasion of his privacy. I have seen him cornered by them only minutes before a vital race, at the very time when he most needs to be left alone. I have sat with him in the quiet of his caravan when he has been feeling dejected and angry with himself after a defeat but has still been unable to relax because of people knocking on the walls, doors and windows.

Few people realize the intensity of Mike's critical self-examination if he has failed to win, or the especially bitter frustration he feels when a machine has let him down. Underneath his happy-go-lucky public manner, he suffers disappointment to an alarmingly low level.

Once, after a race in which the bike had let him down when he was leading, he lapsed into a silence that lasted for an hour. It happened after the 1967 Italian Grand Prix at Monza. This was much more than just another race: the outcome of the world 500 cc championships depended on it. Mike, whose normal determination had been redoubled by his fury at being written off by the Italian newspapers, drove himself to the point of exhaustion in his effort to beat Giacomo Agostini. But with the race in his pocket, and Agostini trailing miles behind, Mike's big Honda broke down. He didn't wait for the end of the race; he strode off to his car and we headed back towards the hotel. The exits from Monza Park were crowded and jammed with cars all making for Milan. Mike couldn't be bothered to wait his turn in the traffic but swung his car off the roadway and sped along the rutted grass verge, hooting furiously at anybody who got in his way.

At the hotel, where we were sharing a room, he maintained his silence. At last he broke it to say with a smile, 'Let's go and get drunk.'

Mike, mercurial in his moods, had slipped out of his feeling of disappointment. In its place he substituted a mood of gaiety. On his way to the bar he signed as many autograph-books as he could. . . .

That night, in the garden restaurant of the Hotel S'Eustorgio at Arcore, near Milan, any of the diners watching Mike could have written him off as a man without emotion. The afternoon's disappointment was gone. He was the life and soul of the party.

The mechanic who had prepared the machine that had broken down was full of self-recrimination, but Mike took him on one side to console him. Then he sent a dozen bottles of champagne to the table where the Japanese team was dining. He joked with them, Indian-wrestled with one and helped another ride into the hotel's goldfish pool.

The party ended when the other guests threatened to call the police because they couldn't get to sleep. Shortly after dawn, when I got up to go to the airport to catch the plane back to London, Mike offered to drive me to Linate. After a hair-raising drive we shook hands, and he said casually, 'It's a bastard, you know.'

'What is?'

'Losing a race like yesterday's.'

It was the first time he had mentioned it; in a way it seemed as if he was thinking aloud. Even though he might appear to have dismissed the episode from his mind, it was obviously still a sore point with him.

I complimented him on not having burdened others with his problems, and he answered, 'There's nothing anybody else can do, so why should I involve my friends in my own misery. It'll be forgotten now. There's always another race. . . .'

People never tire of asking Mike what it was that made him choose the career he did. After all, with the dedication he has applied to racing he could equally well have been an excellent golfer, a good boxer, a successful businessman or a musician. He has dabbled in each of these subjects with more success than is usual in a passing interest.

The question stumps him; his answer is a simplification because there is no real answer. 'It's what I'm best at. There was something inside me that dictated my interest.' He is mystified by this instinct, genuinely astounded that he is superior to any other rider in the world, and is at a loss to explain his superiority or define its roots.

I ask him, 'Why are you better than anybody else?—how do you define the factor that gives you that edge?'

I thought, because I had caught him off guard and relaxed, that the reply would be more revealing. He deliberated the point and came up with this answer.

'Experience. That's all it is. I'm more experienced than anybody else around at the moment. That's what gives me the edge. There's another point, too; I've maintained a standard I set myself years ago. Others have simply fallen behind it, failed to maintain the same level. That, I think, is the only difference.

'Am I more daring than the others? No, I don't think so. As far as I can, I calculate the risks. Balance . . . feel? Well, I'm just like any other man: two arms, a head, two legs. I can't see any advantages there.

'I have often wondered about all this, I've thought deeply about it without coming up with an answer. I suppose that, aside from the experience, there must be *something*—don't ask me what. Maybe it's just our old friend the will to win.'

I asked him, 'Why can't a man of similar weight, near enough the same length of experience, riding a machine that matches yours, get through a corner as safely as you at the same speed?'

'I suppose he should be able to, though it doesn't always work out that way, does it?'

We both knew the answer to that one. The Argentinian rider Benedicto Caldarella, who had given Mike a hard run for his money in the 1964 United States Grand Prix at Daytona, Florida, had tried to copy the champion's style and speed at the Dutch TT four months later. It was almost his last action on a racing-circuit.

Mike was first through the long curve that leads into the straight past the grandstand. The Argentinian was behind him, almost on his tail. Mike swept the MV neatly and quickly—very quickly—through the bend, eased the leaning machine back on to an even keel and urged it down the straight.

Caldarella, copying every move, flowed into the bend on his Gilera.

By rights, and especially as he had so closely followed Mike's style, he should have been through, and away, quite safely. Instead he completely lost control, and the bike swerved off the track and onto the grass, scattering straw from the bales on the opposite side of the circuit as he skimmed them. He kept control but he never recovered, and for the rest of the race couldn't get as close as he had been to Mike.

'I got through there quite safely,' said Mike, 'and without any worries at all. I don't understand why Caldarella didn't.'

For the 25,000 people watching at that particular spot there could have been no doubt that there is a marginal difference between Mike and the others; what it is cannot possibly be defined. I would refute Mike's explanation that it is entirely experience, on the grounds that when he first started racing he had no experience and he was on the winning way even then.

Stan Hailwood's reasoning is more basic than Mike's but no more illuminating. 'The feel for racing was born into him. It's not something that could be learnt—but his experience has enhanced the development of what was already there.'

Bill Ivy, riding for Yamaha, has struggled to fight Mike off and has had the opportunity of watching him on the world's circuits. He sums up the question this way. 'I think the answer lies first and foremost in his will to win; this is why he is so hard to beat. He refuses to give up or even to yield a single inch. If you want to take any ground from him, you really have to earn it. He gets into, through, and out of corners quicker than anybody I have seen; he is amazing.

'Yet he's not the neatest rider. Technically, he does all sorts of things wrong. He sticks his knees and elbows out, his head bobs all over the place on corners. He feels for the corner with his body; he moves about all over the machine until he finds a comfortable position from which he can get the most out of the corner. You can learn a lot from following him, but the point to remember is not to copy him all the way, because if you do you'll most likely find yourself in a lot of trouble.

'Whenever Mike's racing in an event I'm not entered for, I like to go to some corner, or a quick bend, and watch him through. Quite a few of us usually do this, especially at the TT. It's a real eye-opener, because however good you may think you are his speed alters your view.

'His reputation alone is enough to frighten off most people. When Mike joined Honda, Phil Read and I worked under a terrible psychological handicap. First there was Jim Redman to beat, then, if we managed to head him, there was Mike. Can you imagine starting a race with problems like that?'

There is a wonderfully interesting comparison to be drawn between Mike and, say, the top footballers of Britain. Which has the greater individual importance in the eyes of the fans is a hypothetical argument, according to which sport one follows. Mike is at the absolute summit of popularity and adulation in his field, not only in this country but abroad, too. He is watched by something like two million people every season.

The numbers who watch footballers of similar status amount to probably three-quarters of a million. There are players who are national idols, whose every word is greedily swallowed up by their fans; players on whom demands fall far behind those made on Mike. And there are footballers who could never even hope to achieve an equal level of national or international status with Mike. Almost without exception, these players will not give interviews or pose for Press pictures without asking for money; and many of them are awkward and unapproachable.

A sports writer on a British national newspaper said, 'When I first watched Hailwood race, I was amazed at his skill and his daring. The adulation he commands suddenly came clear to me when I watched him; but I was prepared, having had dealings with our other top sportsmen—mainly soccer players—to find that he would be difficult.

'I couldn't have been more wrong. I went to see him; he was busy, really busy, but he managed to find time to talk to me. He was charming and patient, despite the fact that he was talking to a man who knew very little about the sport.

'What was more refreshing to me was that he didn't start asking for money. If one of our soccer players was in the same position, a world champion nine times over on his own merits, I wouldn't have got even a smile without it costing at least ten quid.

'If Mike had the same mind as a footballer, in the business sense, he would be worth a fortune. I don't know how much he earns—and whatever it is, he deserves every penny—but he could easily have doubled it by asking money for interviews. If he had, though, he certainly wouldn't now be commanding the respect he does. As it is, he leaves a tremendous impression; no wonder he's so popular among newsmen.'

2 Pangbourne

To young Hailwood, the lush, neatly trimmed lawns of Pangbourne Nautical College looked ideal for grass-track racing. The thought would have given the gardener apoplexy; it would also have worried the Captain Superintendent of the day, for the riding of motor-cycles in term-time was forbidden. This regulation was the most disturbing aspect of Mike's schooling at Pangbourne; not that he took much notice of it—as soon as he got home at the week-ends he spent long hours on his motor-bike.

Pangbourne—fees £537 a year—is an independent public school in the upper Thames Valley, near Reading. The college was built on the eastern spur of the Berkshire Downs and extends over some 230 acres. Its aims are to promote self-reliance and a smart and alert bearing, and to prepare its boys for careers as officers in the Royal and Merchant Navies. It has produced, by its own standards, one notable failure. . . .

I asked Captain Superintendent Patrick Lewis, CBE, Royal Navy (retired), for information about Mike's schooling, and this is what he told me.

'From the very moment Hailwood arrived at the school he announced his intention of becoming a motor-cycle- and motor-racing-driver. I fear that the academic side of school life held very little appeal for him, either at his prep school or here. As a result he occupied a rather lowly place in the bottom stream of the school.

'His only real interests and abilities were for work with his hands, and he found an outlet for them in the Model Club here at school and in his father's workshops at home. He was a more than useful boxer and represented the College at his weight. He had a term in the choir and also joined the Band, and he belonged to the Stamp Club. But fairly soon it became clear that on the academic side he was not going to achieve any worthwhile success, and with the Captain's agreement his father decided to withdraw him and let his apparent bent for the practical side of life have full rein.'

When Mike left, the then Captain wrote: 'I do not feel that his time here has been a "dead loss". Far from it, but I doubt if he would have achieved much in the academic field. I have no doubt, however, that he will make a success in the practical field which appeals to him.'

Two of Mike's contemporaries were Atlantic oarsman John Ridgeway, and John Guthrie, who sailed the Atlantic in 1967. Before him were rugger internationals D. R. de Stacpoole, H. C. C. Laird, D. St Clair Ford and Rex Willis. Then there was Admiral Sir Frank Hopkins, KCB, DSO, DSC, Commander-in-Chief Portsmouth until 1967; General Sir Norman Tailyour, KCB, DSO and Bar, Commandant General, Royal Marines; and Major-General Sir John Willoughby, who recently retired as GOC Middle East. Now Pangbourne can add to its roll of honour the name of Mike Hailwood, MBE. For even if he did leave without having scaled any notable academic pinnacles, the College is still proud to claim that he was educated there.

'If I hadn't reacted as sharply as I did—and still do—to enforced discipline and routine, and if I hadn't been such an idle so-and-so, I might now be Lieutenant-Commander Hailwood, RN,' said Mike. 'I spent my early years dreaming about life at sea. More than anything I wanted to be a naval officer. I pictured myself shouting orders from the bridge of a warship.

'The trouble was that a vast amount of study lay between me and my ambitions, a lot of hard work on what to me were dull subjects. Academic pursuits were definitely not my strong point, and it didn't take the College too long to catch on.

'After a couple of years at a nursery school near my home at Goring-on-Thames, Stan sent me to a prep school at Purton Stoke, near Newbury. At six years of age I was living away from home at this boarding-school, trying to do all the things that were supposed to shape me as a future gentleman, ready to ease myself into high social circles. I had piano lessons and learnt to ride. I struggled through eight years at Purton Stoke.

'Believe it or not, it was while I was there that I had my first experience of handling motor-cycles. When I was seven, Stan bought me a mini-bike—it was basically a Royal Enfield, powered by a 100-cc engine and with a top speed of around thirty. I also had a small car—again with a 100-cc engine—but that wasn't nearly so much fun as the bike. Best of all, at the time, was an ex-RAF Link trainer, a flight-simulator used to teach service pilots the fundamentals of flying before they were competent to leave the ground.

'It's strange how those playthings I had at seven have formed the basis of my life: a career of racing motor-cycles, a brief spell in cars and an interest in flying in my spare time.

'But don't look on that as being the beginning of my racing career. That motor-bike to me was just a novelty, a super-toy that none of my friends could match. I didn't even play the usual childish game of pretending to be a champion—I didn't know the names of any, in fact.

'Stan had given me the chance to choose for myself where I would go to continue my education, and unfortunately for him—and for the Nautical College—I decided on Pangbourne. It was the uniform as much as anything else that attracted me. I imagined it made me look a grown man, a real sailor.

'Before I moved to Pangbourne to be steeped in its naval tradition, Stan took me up to London to be kitted out with the necessary uniforms. I strode out of the tailor's feeling pretty pleased with myself, in a navy blue double-breasted uniform, a peaked cap—with a white cover for summer—and three pairs of shiny black shoes. Fourteen years old and a man already! I must have been a dreadfully cocky little brat.

'A friend of mine, who was already at Pangbourne, told me I wouldn't have to learn Latin. I was delighted; that made me even keener to go. He was right, too: I didn't learn Latin. But it didn't help much. Mathematics horrified me. History bored me stiff. Only French and Geography held any interest for me at all; they were the only academic subjects I was any good at.

'But the worst thing was that I was lumbered with seamanship, sailing and navigation, which were a complete mystery to me. I realize now that you have to be dedicated to become a naval officer. At the time I thought it would be a bit of fun. I must have horrified all those boys who were born to go to sea. They sweated and strained away at it, frightened to death of not being able to follow in their fathers' footsteps. But I soon found it boring; and once the rot had set in my father was paying out good money just to see me listed as bottom of my class in every end-of-term report.

'As time went on I got worse and worse, and Stan played stink because I couldn't force myself to show any interest. Hailwood the officer and gentleman was simply not taking shape. The more all the others looked the part, the less I did, and the less I wanted to.

'I had no idea what I did want to be in life, but I certainly didn't relish the thought of becoming a seaman any more. My life was a never-ending series of crossroads. At one stage I thought I'd like to be a marine, but that was only because I was stirred by the military music played by the College band.

'The only really enjoyable bright spots during those years were my consuming interests in boxing and music. I threw all my energies into both these sidelines whenever I could. I fought for the College and became the champion at my weight; but the boxing began by accident. I was chosen for one of the rugger teams, and in only my second game I took a terrible kick in the mouth. It was hard enough to make me realize that rugby was not going to be my forte. So I looked for a manly way out of the team. I didn't want to show myself up as a coward, so I chose boxing as the alternative. At least it was man-to-man combat, one sport where you weren't leapt upon by hordes of kicking, punching lunatics who didn't care too much whether they punted the ball or the man. I worked it out that I might well lose a couple of teeth, but I wouldn't lose face; and it was up to me to make sure I didn't get a beating.

'It turned out that at last I had found something at which I could shine, something I could master. In fourteen bouts I won thirteen and shared a split decision in the last fight I had. I think I might have won that one and retired with a hundred-per-cent record, but I was in my last term by then and couldn't be bothered to train.

'My being a good boxer, and a frequent winner, seemed to placate Stan. He had been a good boxer himself in his youth, and as I seemed to be a chip off the old block he apparently overlooked the other side of my school life. It didn't get me out of lessons, though; I had to train in between or after classes. I've still never been fitter in my life; it was arduous work, but I'm sure it gave me a sound foundation for my strength. I had nightly sessions punching out all my frustrations on the heavy bag, I skipped and shadow-boxed until my legs ached, but it was all to prove valuable when I took up motor-cycle racing.

'Another, more immediate, benefit I got from boxing was that the College bullies stopped taking the mickey out of me. I used to suffer agonies because of their baiting. I had a peculiar sort of accent, a mixture of Cockney and Northern. I used to pronounce my name "Oilwood", and it became my nickname. Everybody at College used to call me by it—until I started winning the boxing contests. Then all the jibes came to a stop; they didn't call me that to my face.

'I must have been a furious little fighter. I remember knocking one of my opponents stone-cold to the canvas. I'm sure now that my will to win dates from Pangbourne. The feeling seems to have been with me since those days; I have a massive urge to win at whatever I attempt. I think it's an important part of any sportsman's make-up. Without it, the margin of skill becomes so narrow as not to matter; but it's the will that can lift you out of yourself. In any sort of contest between men of roughly equal skills the one with the will to win should come out tops every time. The point is not only to win, but to win well and convincingly. The day I stop winning like that is the day I will quit racing.

'The other main interest of my schooldays has remained with me right up to the present day. Music is still my second love, after motorcycle racing. After learning to play the piano at Purton Stoke, I was taught a variety of instruments at Pangbourne. Music filled in the gaps between boxing and lessons, and I soon picked up the knack of getting sounds out of the drums, bugle and fife. I was drafted into the College band and was the only member who could play all the instruments.

'On the side we ran an unofficial jazz-band, and I was in my element thumping out tunes on the piano in the gym. After the piano I tried my hand at the cornet, banjo, guitar and clarinet.

'Whatever charms music might have had, the 'Reveille' bugle-blast at dawn wasn't one of them. In the blocks where we were housed, the duty bugler used to blast us out of bed every morning at around 6.30. It was a heathen way to get us out of bed, but an effective one. It was also the prelude to a horrid hour of dashing round the block in singlet and shorts, whatever the weather, followed by an icy cold shower.

'Nobody should ever believe that public-school life is for the idle rich. It may be highly expensive, but it toughens you up and shakes you out of any lethargy you may have inherited from wealthy parents. I'm sure that the boys at Pangbourne were every bit as tough as any at the schools in the East End of London. The only difference is that when a public-schoolboy punches somebody on the nose he probably says, "Excuse me, but I'm afraid you've left me no alternative."

'A feeling of independence is bred into public-schoolboys. You're away from home, living in common-rooms and dormitories, out of range of the fussing of doting parents. There's nobody to run to if you're in trouble, no parental shoulder to cry on, nobody to soothe away schoolboy hurts. You're on your own, and this, without doubt, forces you to grow up quicker. You have to—it's a simple matter of sink or swim. A boy who remains soft at a public school probably suffers far more than he would at a secondary modern or grammar school. You can at least escape some of the agony if you're living at home, but when you live, eat and sleep in the close confines of a public school, escape is impossible.

'The rough discipline at the College terrified all the cadets. There was organized corporal punishment meted out by the masters, but it was nothing compared with what was dished out by the boys themselves, the senior cadets. If you broke a rule—and there were so many of them, both written and unwritten, that it was impossible not to—you were severely dealt with by the older boys. Their idea of punishment was merciless, far more cruel than the simple crack across the backside from a master. I would far sooner have been given a hiding by one of the staff than by one of the senior cadets.

'I took one dreadful beating at Pangbourne; one that I am sure was among the heftiest ever handed out there. I have never forgotten it, and I don't suppose I ever shall. In a typical bit of schoolboy fooling around, I'd been flicking paper pellets in one of the corridors. I was seen by a senior boy, but he said nothing to me at the time, and I thought I'd got away with it. Later I wished he had told one of the masters. . . .

'That night, when I was in the dormitory getting ready for bed, a senior came in to see me and told me to go to another room upstairs. I knew what to expect and there was nothing I could—or was prepared to—do about it. It wasn't written into College regulations, but it was still the law. The self-appointed punishment committee had decided that my offence had earned me a beating. Somebody stood guard at the door while I was told to drop my trousers and forced to lie on my stomach across a table. Then one of the beefier seniors lashed me across the buttocks with a steel-shafted golf-club.

'I still shiver when I think about that club whistling down again and again. Six times it was smashed down onto my backside. The stinging pain never seemed to let up.

'After it was all over one of the boys said curtly, "Don't do it again—or you'll get more." As if I needed reminding after a whipping like that. I had the weals for days afterwards.

'I'm convinced that the masters knew about the punishment committee but didn't want to curb it. I suppose they thought the senior boys knew everything that was going on, and that they were the people best fitted to stop trouble in their own manner, however barbarous that might be.

'If you can earn punishment as severe as what I was forced to suffer for an offence so minor, I shudder to think what would have happened to somebody who had done something really serious.

'I was fifteen when it happened; the boys who handed out the beatings were usually around seventeen or eighteen. Their favourite method of dealing with offenders was to lash them with a knotted rope. I can't imagine why I qualified for a beating with a golf club; probably because I was more of a sportsman than a potential seaman. The done thing was to accept a beating with a stiff upper lip—and leave with a sore backside. To complain officially about a beating would only have got you into more trouble.

'I suppose this was looked upon by the masters as an essential part of the character-shaping process, the basis of the British Public-School system. Take your punishment like a man, say nothing, be phlegmatic, and unmoved—and, above all, don't cry.

'Most of the seamanship we were taught was the dry-land version of sailing. Occasionally one of the ex-Royal-Navy masters would take us on the river, where we were shown the knack of handling large whaling-boats. With a crew of eight to twelve we used to row up and down the river, pulling massive oars with puny, twig-like arms. Then, having survived that, and having worked up an enormous appetite, our next problem was to live through the ship's biscuits we were issued with. They were appalling: two-inch-square naval biscuits, like concrete chippings and chock full of weevils. You had to knock them against something even harder to evict the weevils. The biscuits were so hard I'm sure they were First-World-War surplus.

'There was precious little to do at Pangbourne other than study; the village near by was deathly quiet and there was no fun to be had there. I remember once being so bored with life that I decided to walk to Reading and back, something like sixteen miles. To walk that far you have to be at the depths of boredom—and you have to be fit. I was both.

'One vivid memory of life at Pangbourne caught up with me years after I'd left. A London model girl, Sally Noel, used to ride her horse round the school playing-fields when she was about fourteen. She was often dressed in the shortest, tightest shorts, and stirred feelings in us that we didn't fully understand. But the masters, full of protective instincts both for the girl and for their cadets, regularly asked her to leave and ride her horse somewhere else. I met Sally ten years later, and discovered in the course of conversation that she was the girl. She told me that at the time she couldn't understand why she was ordered from the grounds.

'While I was at Pangbourne I had my first taste of real speed, when my mother used to collect me every third week to take me home for a couple of days. She had an XK120 Jaguar which she used to drive to the College from home—and I drove it part of the way back. As soon as we got on to the lonelier roads we swapped places, and I went behind the wheel. I was fourteen, and I could just about see the road between the top of the dashboard and the rim of the steering-wheel. You could hardly see me, I was so small. Anybody passing would have thought there was nobody driving, or that the car had a left-hand drive. I could scarcely reach the pedals, and I had to half-sit, half-stand behind the wheel; but I used to rush along at sixty and seventy miles an hour, scaring the life out of myself. I suppose the speed bug had bitten me even then, but I wasn't aware of it; I just looked on it as great fun.

'But Stan hadn't sent me to Pangbourne to learn how to drive Jaguars. He must have seen the writing on the wall, because every one of my end-of-term reports showed my lack of interest. I was bottom of the class with notable consistency. I tried hard enough, but I didn't have the will-power to stir myself out of my lethargy. Once I had fallen into it there was no way out except the obvious one—to leave the College.

'Stan must have realized this, and he must have been very disappointed and very weary of telling me off for being such a poor pupil. Inevitably the end came after two and a half years. Stan accepted that it was all a waste of money and discussed it with the superintendent, Captain Skinner, who had recognized my lack of interest and my increasing boredom. Between them they agreed that the best course for me would be through the exit door. I can't say I was sorry. When they told me I skipped all the way back to my dormitory in Harbinger Division, my home for more than two years, packed my bags and simply walked out of public-school life without a single regret.

'I know Stan didn't share my happiness; he desperately wanted me to go the full course and emerge at the end of it as a successful young gentleman. I knew he was fairly well off, and I thought I'd be able to sponge off him for a few years until I had made up my mind what I wanted to do. But he had different ideas. I was just turned sixteen when he sent me away to work on the shop-floor at the Triumph motor-cycle factory at Meriden. I'd had a spell in the family business, but it hadn't worked out too well. Stan knew one of the bosses at Triumph and he arranged the job for me, but it wasn't the usual sort of old-pals act. I didn't even get half-way up the ladder—I was stuck right down at the bottom end of it. Stan fixed it so that I got all the dirty jobs: sweeping the floors, brewing-up and running errands. Then I was put on the assembly line, and a more boring, tedious job I cannot imagine. Anybody who works on that side of motor-cycle building deserves every penny he earns; personally, I couldn't stand it.

'At first I lived in a cheap hotel, then in digs. But I was very much on my own again. One day was just like another. It was my old childhood enemy—routine—all over again. I must have put a million engines and bikes together on that assembly line, but after all that experience I couldn't even have begun to piece one together on my own. And it's as big a mystery to me now as it was then.

'The months dragged by. I felt like an automaton, mechanically, absent-mindedly sticking bits of this, that and the other on to a unit as it rolled by. I was transferred after a while into the experimental section, where they were working on production racers, but it sparked no interest whatever in me. When I looked at the engines I saw only steel pipes, wires and castings that looked like one of those unfathomable Chinese puzzles. Whatever they told me about them failed to sink in.

'Occasionally I went to Brands or Mallory Park with a cousin to watch the racing. It occurred to me in passing that it might be fun to have a go. Only fun—nothing more. I had no ambitions to become a professional. It was very much a pastime to me.

'I used to travel to and from work on a 250 cc AJS I had bought, but I never raced against the "cowboys" who would overtake me on my way to the factory. The urge to race along the main roads was never in me; the high-street contests seemed pointless, stupid and dangerous. It's a view I still hold, by the way.

'The attraction of racing, in the proper places, was the thrill of being able to beat somebody in actual competition, to take on somebody who was equally matched. I don't think speed as such has ever excited me; as a means to an end, though, it's given me plenty of satisfaction. Linked with fierce competition, it can fill you with a kind of enjoyable fear. The only time you really notice the pace is when you're wrapped up in a hard dice with somebody and you're approaching a difficult corner side by side. It's the cat-and-mouse sensation of wondering if the other man will back down before you do; it borders on bravado.

'The spirit for this sort of contest grew up with me from my schooldays. I had been in so many teams, in so many direct contests in the ring, that my will to win had developed very strongly. The personal satisfaction of beating somebody in an equal match is the real basis of motor-cycle racing, or, for that matter, of any competitive sport. Know-

Top: This is how it all started. Mike, aged seven, bruising the lawn outside his Oxford home.

Left: And showing he can ride horses, too.

Below: The budding Naval officer aboard a 197 James on which he used to practice in a near-by field.

FEROD

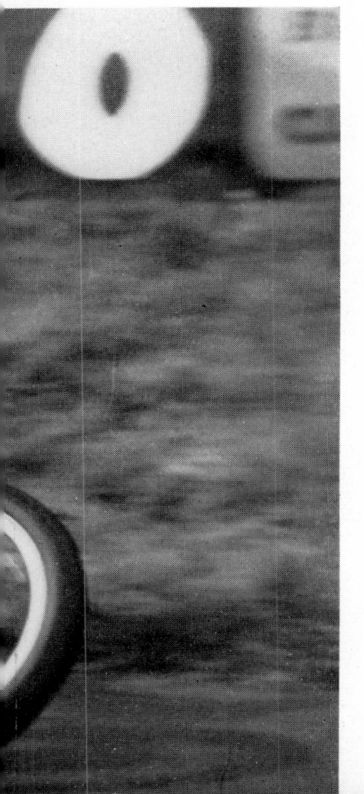

Top left: It ain't much, but it's home. Mike, with Mr and Mrs Hailwood, at their Oxford mansion.

Top right: Mike in his first season; Castle Combe, 1957.

Left: Mike, his style beginning to show, throws his 175 MV round Oliver's Mount, Scarborough. A few minutes later he fell off!

His first TT. And his third breakdown in practice at the same spot.

ing that you can beat the best in the world, and then doing it, is a marvellous feeling. Even when the riders have a get-together at a hotel after a race, the card-games we play become fiercely competitive, because the will to win, even at a friendly game, is just as strong as it is on the circuit.

'You can say that it's only a game, but the loser still gets annoyed that he hasn't won. The essential thing is that to *win* is all-important; to spend your life in second place is not really much of an achievement. The ambition *must* be to win, and to win as convincingly as possible; friendships should, and do, stand aside in my sport. It's a rough business and there's no room for sentiment. I don't ask any quarter and I don't give any. On the circuit it's a case of every man for himself; let up for only an instant and you're a runner-up.

'The one really serious dispute I've had with Stan came after he thought I'd let him down. I hadn't been racing long—I was still only seventeen—and we had bought, largely on his initiative, John Surtees's fabulous NSU.

'I stood a good chance of winning the 250 cc race at Silverstone on it, but in the 125 cc event I fell off. I made it back to the pits, but I could hardly walk; my ankle was hurting terribly, and I was in genuine agony. Stan told me not to be so soft and to get on the NSU. I argued with him and refused, the ankle was too painful. He flew into a terrible rage, the worst I'd ever seen him in. He started throwing spanners about and shouting at me, but I wouldn't ride. He wouldn't talk to me and, after another row at home, he threw me out of the house.

'He didn't know, nor did I until I went to hospital, that I had broken the ankle. I thought it was a severe sprain. I didn't go home for two weeks, and Stan spent the time looking for me to apologize, after he'd found out the results of the X-ray.

'I hid myself away at Bill Lacey's house until Stan found out and came to see me. I felt then that Stan was pushing me too hard, but I was an idle item and probably needed shoving. At the time I was entering for as many as ten events in a week-end.

'In those early days, Stan worked like a Trojan to make sure everything moved smoothly and efficiently. I couldn't have had a better, keener manager. Maybe he sees in me what he would have liked to be himself. He used to play hell with me for turning out in scruffy leathers or worn boots. When he'd been racing he'd always worn a clean white overall, and he saw no reason why I shouldn't always be well turned out. Even when I was twenty-one he used to warn me sternly not to be home late if I was going for a night out; I knew I was in dire trouble if I defied him, so I never did. It was hard for me to appreciate then that he was only doing what public school had failed to do. He was instilling some sort of order into my life, holding me in check and preventing me from running wild.

'I suppose that because I'd lived away from home since I was a toddler I grew less reliant on family ties. Instead of becoming more of a father, in the generally accepted sense, Stan became more and more of a friend.

'Nowadays whenever we meet people Stan always introduces me as his kid brother. I suppose racing has aged me so much and caused me to lose so much hair I *look* like his younger brother.'

3 First Steps

Easter Monday, 22 April 1957. A nervous son, a proud father and a chauffeur swing off the Chester road towards Oulton Park, the picturesque racing-circuit in the heart of the flat Cheshire countryside. Stan Hailwood's chauffeur edges the Bentley through the noisy crowds to find a parking-place in the paddock.

Mike Hailwood, now a tousle-haired, fresh-faced seventeen-year-old, is arriving for his first race against some of the motor-cycle giants of the day. The Bentley, the millionaire father, the trappings of luxury, make this surely the most impressive entrance ever for a hopeful debutant in the rough-and-ready business of two-wheel racing.

There was not too much confidence, and a lot of nervousness, in the boy who, in the course of the next few months, was to be hailed as a future champion. The heights he was to climb were still in the dim distance, even if the ambition to scale them was already present in his mind. His entrance might have given him the look of a pampered, spoilt boy, but nothing could have been further from the truth, as subsequent events proved.

Mike surveyed the chaotic scene. Bikes in pieces, oil-cans, engines stripped down and laid out like steel jigsaw puzzles. Men crouched over the parts—men who could have been either riders or mechanics for all Mike knew. He recognized none of them. He had no idols, no heroes. With typical indifference, he had not followed the usual beginner's habit of choosing a style to copy, a rider to model himself on.

The men all appeared much older than they actually were: they had the look of men who are accustomed to living with the threat of death or serious injury. When they looked back at the boy who stared at them, they saw only one more inquisitive youngster, like so many others who swarm into the paddock and around the machines whenever they can. Certainly they could have seen no threat to their own chances in this diffident seventeen-year-old.

A telegram arrived from two friends in Vancouver. They offered good wishes and added, with more confidence than Mike himself could muster, HOME FIRST. Mechanics hired by Stan Hailwood put the finishing touches to Mike's borrowed 125 cc MV. How Stan managed to persuade Bill Webster to lend him the MV is still a mystery.

The bike—No. 36—stripped of a fairing and showing its meticulously clean skeleton, was wheeled out to the grid in front of a grandstand packed with Bank Holiday crowds. Mike was given a passing mention in the pre-race commentary as 'the youngest man in the race'. Embarrassed by his shiny new leathers, helmet, goggles and boots, alongside those well-worn and oily sets of his more experienced opponents, sat self-consciously on the MV. In front of him were the big names: Cecil Sandford, Dudley Edlin, Bill Webster, Fron Purslow, Dave Chadwick.

When the six-lap fourth event got under way, Mike was swallowed up in the rush of experience. He struggled through, trying to find his lines through the corners, sometimes going slower than he should have done, at other times travelling faster than his limited experience justified. But he stayed on the machine, even if the journey was at times alarming to him.

Predictably, Sandford won, with Edlin and Chadwick placed. Mike steered the MV into eleventh place. The first hurdle was behind him. He had been baptized and he had learnt something about the hurly-burly of racing against the professionals.

Mike, smiling at the memory of his first outing, said, 'I just put my head down and went. People were passing me all over the place, and when I tried to keep up with them I got in some awful tangles. Stan had told me to ride my own race and forget the others, and that's what I did.'

'How could I best describe it? Well, I was precisely what I was; a seventeen-year-old trying to mix it with older, much more experienced riders. The thing that horrifies me about the whole business is that I must have looked a real sight with my brand new leathers and everything. Everybody else around me seemed to look so well worn, battle-hardened. I must have stood out like a sore thumb. I might not have been noticeable for my efforts but I bet I was the best-dressed bloke there. Unfortunately there were no prizes for that.

'I wasn't at all disappointed that I only got an eleventh place; in fact I was dead chuffed at finishing at all. The important thing is that the race taught me a lot, and I knew I had a long way to go, even if I had no idea at the time that I would go as far as I have done. I don't think

I had any particular ambition even then to make racing my life. It still seemed a good hobby, something I could do to let off steam.

'I was lucky that Stan was enough keen to support me. He helped me quite a bit when I first started. Then, when I started winning a few races and picking up prize-money and start-money, he made me put the loot towards the machinery and the travelling expenses. He made it plain that he would help me to get going, but that once I was into the credit side it would be up to me to look after myself and my finances.'

S. M. B. Hailwood, ACU licence-holder No. 1786, member of the Oxford Ixion Motor-Cycle Club, packed the once-worn leathers into his father's car and was driven off into the 1957 season. His career was taking shape; within less than a week the fact would be publicly recognized . . . .

Mike's crowded scrapbooks provide the historical background to his life: yellow-edged newspaper clippings, crinkly programmes and fading photographs. His increasing reputation is reflected by the increasing size of the clippings. At the start of the first book he rates half a dozen lines in local papers—and towards the end of the last there are lengthy articles from such non-motor-cycle papers as the *Sunday Times* and *Daily Telegraph* spilling across the wide pages. He has been praised, criticized, dissected and examined, not only in England but all over the world.

Page 3 of that first leather-bound scrapbook records Mike's real arrival on the racing scene. Oulton Park had come and gone with little more to show for it than a lesson from the other riders on how it should be done. But that page shows that on Saturday, 27 April 1957 a national motor-cycle race meeting was held at Castle Combe, organized by the Wessex Centre.

Stuck across the face of the pea-green programme is a telegram jointly signed by Stan Hailwood's business associate Bert North and the well-known rider Bill Webster, the man who helped Mike so much in the beginning. It was addressed to: *Michael Hailwood, Highmoor Hall, Nettlebed, Henley-on-Thames*, and the text went: CONGRATULATIONS ON YOUR EXCELLENT PERFORMANCE TODAY. REMEMBER YOUR FATHER'S MOTTO: WE HAVEN'T STARTED YET.

That day, only five days after making his debut in racing, Mike had clinched a fourth place out of a field of thirty-one entrants in the 125 race, and was lapping only fractionally slower than the second man.

Then, in the 250 event two races later, he earned himself a fifth place, again in a list of thirty-one riders. Each of the races was liberally sprinkled with hardened professionals, but the precocious youngster refused to be impressed by reputations.

A single-column story in a local paper, topped by a picture of the youthful Hailwood, recorded: 'A seventeen-year-old Oxford boy, Michael Hailwood, sprang the surprise of the day . . .' The same paper, using precisely the same photograph—there were so few of him around at the time—gave him space again after another national meeting at Blandford Camp, Dorset. But if the face was the same, the story at least was different.

It was the day Mike says he will never forget—Whit Monday, 10 June 1957. Mike won the 125 event after leading all the way, and the official race report issued to the newspapers by the track's Press officer said: 'We have a feeling we shall be hearing more of this young man.' The perceptive official didn't have long to wait. In the newly introduced 50 cc class Mike scored a third, and then came a fifth place in the 250 cc event.

Blandford brought Mike another first—his first national newspaper headline. It read: MICHAEL HAILWOOD SPRINGS SURPRISE, and reported: '. . . It is a twisting, winding circuit that demands the highest degree of riding skill, and there was great excitement amongst the 40,000 spectators that a seventeen-year-old boy, on his first outing at the course, should beat so many of the older, experienced and even factory-mounted riders.' In the flood of letters of congratulation that poured through Mike's letter-box was one from the MV Agusta distributor, Ron Harris. He predicted: 'From what I have seen of your riding ability there will be plenty more wins to follow in the future.'

A battered and buckled silver watchstrap, anchored into the scrapbook by two slips of adhesive paper, is Mike's reminder that racing can be painful, too. At Scarborough, on the tricky Oliver's Mount circuit, his handlebars touched another rider's and they were both thrown off at around 90 m.p.h. Mike dislocated a thumb and gashed an arm and a knee. A doctor banned him from racing for six weeks—but three weeks after the spill he was back in the saddle to take two second places at Silverstone. In only three months' racing since his début, he had never been placed lower than fifth.

Mounting confidence, more experience and a tremendous will to win whatever the odds forced Mike to go quicker and to take more risks. With four firsts, three seconds, three thirds and three fourths in only eighteen races he got his international licence. Normally it takes about eighteen months to reach this status.

Back he went to Oulton Park for his first international meeting on 3 August. His plan was to follow up this meeting by going on to Ireland for the classic Ulster Grand Prix. . . . This time at Oulton Park he knew who the riders were, and what mechanics looked like. And when they looked at him now, instead of the shy spectator of the Easter Monday meeting they recognized the boy who was earning himself rave reports and a reputation for being a difficult man to beat.

The MVs had now taken on the full professional look; they looked trimmer under a full fairing which had painted on the side *For Love of the Sport*. A sparkling new van, with *Nil Desperandum* and *Ecurie Sportive* emblazoned under a Union Jack all over its length, was used to transport them to meetings throughout the country.

Against international opposition Mike notched a third place in the 125 race and second in the 50 event. Then came the event that to Mike was all-important—the 250 cc race. Taking part in it were John Surtees and Cecil Sandford.

'I was really in with the big boys now,' said Mike, 'and I suppose I was full of myself. I'd had a terrific season up to then and I was afraid of nobody. Reputations didn't count for anything to me. My 250 was very competitive and I felt I was raring to go, ready to take anybody on. I certainly had plenty of confidence; a bit different from my first race. My leathers looked nicely worn, too.

'When I sat across the bike on the grid I had a good look round. John Surtees was there—he was the 250 world champion. Then there was Cecil Sandford, the 125 champion and TT winner. I saw no reason why I couldn't beat them both. There was no point in being frightened of them. Once you start thinking that way, you've lost.

'John and I both got good starts, and I was holding on to his tail like grim death. Then I made a fatal error: I tried to go through as fast as John at Lodge Corner, not the best place to take a risk. The front wheel touched the grass verge and the bike humped me overboard. I shot dramatically up in the air, levelled off at about fifteen feet, then made a heavy landing on my shoulder. I broke my collar-bone and severely dented my ego. It was nobody's fault but mine. I ignored my father's advice to take it easy and not let my successes go to my head. I was, shall we say, a little impetuous. When I found myself actually giving John Surtees a run for his cash I couldn't resist the temptation to have a good go.

'If ever anybody felt a complete fool it was me. One good thing came out of it—it taught me another lesson. I was, I think, probably being a bit cheeky trying to hold my own with John at that point and I got my bottom smacked. But a greater punishment for me was that I had to withdraw from the Ulster. I was laid up for weeks. Stan gave me a fair-sized lashing for being so daft and for trying to run before I could really walk in the business.

'The lessons were coming in hard and fast, too. However well I did, right there among the pats on the back were words of warning and valuable advice both from my father and from his friends, who had forgotten more about racing than I would ever know. I'm lucky to have had such help at a critical time, a time when I most needed it.

'For instance, I had a dreadful habit when I first started of constantly swivelling round on the bike and looking back down the road to see who was following and how close they were. In fact, I probably spent more time looking backwards than I did watching where I was going. So when I won at Brands Hatch—and set up a new record in the 200 cc race—I still got a kick up the backside from Ron Harris. It seemed harsh at the time, especially when I thought I had done so well, but when I look back I realize it was quite timely.'

Mike thumbed the pages of the scrapbook, pointed to a letter from Ron Harris and said, 'How about that? If that wouldn't make a young rider keep his sense of proportion, what would?'

The letter read:

> I felt sorry that I had spoken a few criticisms to you as I felt that I might possibly have depreciated from the elation you must have felt after your splendid riding. However, I think you know me well enough to know that I only spoke entirely in your own interests as I have been watching you very closely and I am deeply interested in seeing you progress.
>
> It is only because you have outstanding talent that you are worthy of criticism or advice, and I do hope you accepted it in the spirit it was intended.

Said Mike, 'How about that? Now comes the sting in the tail.' He turned the page. . . .

The letter went on:

> If I may reiterate without becoming a bore, I would like to suggest that you try and rid yourself of the habit of constantly turning your head and looking for the opposition. I can assure you that you are

losing valuable fractions of seconds in so doing and, in addition to the time factor, it is also dangerous and you may well run into a tumble. It is far better to concentrate entirely on the job in hand and, in these short-distance events, ride your own race without worrying what the other man is doing.

I hope my remarks did not cause any damper on your well-merited elation after your fine riding. Believe me I would not waste my breath on many of the riders and I am sure you fully appreciate this.

The scrapbooks are full of such letters and telegrams mixing congratulation with criticism, dating from Mike's early formative years in racing. He treasures every one of them; for the criticism was constructive.

Stan Hailwood, straw-hatted in the tanning sunshine of Cannes, put his hand across his forehead to shade his eyes from the glare and squinted towards a sea full of bobbing heads and romping bathers.

Skimming across the water, towed by a sleek speedboat, was Mike, water-skiing. 'There he is,' said Stan, pointing; 'he took to water-skiing as though he had been doing it all his life. He's got such a tremendous feel for balance. . . .' No sooner had he made this observation than Mike's arms started flailing, he wobbled from side to side, first on one leg then on the other, and finally went skidding and cartwheeling over the surface like a flat stone, to vanish in an explosion of spray. Stan stood up, to make sure Mike surfaced, and went on, 'As I was saying, he's got fine balance. And as I was going to add, before that display of accidental gymnastics we've just been privileged to watch, the trouble is that he can't perfect anything quickly enough for his liking. He wants to run before he can walk. It's always been the same. He's so determined and so resilient that he learns something from lessons like that one. He has a knack for not doing the same thing wrong twice.

'It was the same when he first started racing. I used to drum it into his head that he must go his own way and let the others do as they pleased. It took a while for the advice to sink in and, because he ignored it at first, he had a couple of tumbles. But he *did* learn.'

There are no blurred edges to Stan Hailwood's memories of Mike's development. Every tiny incident, every venture, success and failure, is as crystal to him now as it was when it first happened. He is a walking authority on the champion.

He chuckled over a photograph he had taken when Mike was seven. It showed Mike, complete with crash helmet, ripping up one of the lawns of their Oxford home on his tiny motor-bike. He said, 'I didn't dream then that he would ever turn out to be a world champion. He wasn't a prodigy, just a kid enjoying himself on a sophisticated toy.

'When he was at Pangbourne Nautical College I used to collect him after church parade on Sundays and take him home. I bought him a 'Trials' James and he couldn't wait to get home and jump on it. For hours on end he would ride it round a field we had close by the house. It used to drive the neighbours mad, having to listen to a machine with no silencer disturbing their Sunday quiet. He was fourteen at the time.

'I watched very critically, and it began to dawn on me that he wasn't just playing about, he was serious and good. I had the idea, from what I had seen, that he might make a good rider. But, I repeat, I certainly didn't see a future world-beater in him; and if anybody had told me he was to be a champion within five years I'd have laughed at him.

'Unknown to Mike, I ran a test on him. One of the boys who worked for me was an excellent grass-track racer. I sent him up to the oval Mike had worn in the field—it was about twelve hundred yards round—and asked him to put the James round it as fast as he could. When I timed him he was slower than Mike.

'He was flabbergasted. He told me he had been having a real go and couldn't lap any quicker.'

It was interesting to hear Stan's version of what happened after Mike left Pangbourne and went into the family business, King's of Oxford.

'It was no use, no use at all. He didn't like the humdrum life of business and the routine that goes with it. He soon got fed up.

'I didn't mollycoddle him. He may have been the boss's son but he started where any other newcomer did, on the motor-bike and float delivering machines to the station and running errands for all and sundry.

'The trip to the station usually took about fifteen minutes, but with Mike it began to take an hour, then more. The foreman reported to me that Mike was playing truant somewhere along the line. I taxed him about it, and he admitted he'd been getting bored and pushed off for a dice round the town.

'I wasn't having that, whether he was my son or not. I packed him off to Triumph at Birmingham, where he thought he was going to get a job as a tester. But I expect he's told you all about that.

'His impatience was enormous. He's the same now. If there's any routine involved Mike doesn't want to know about it; I can't imagine what sort of a naval officer he would have been if he'd gone through with Pangbourne. Routine leaves him cold.

'He wasn't happy with his lot at Triumph and he pestered me to let him try his hand at racing. I told him he was too young and that it was difficult to find a machine small enough and suitable for his needs. But he was obviously so keen that I gave way and decided to help him as much as I could. A friend of mine, Bill Webster who lived at Crewe in Cheshire, had a pair of 125 cc MVs, a single-knocker and a double-knocker. I asked him to sell me one of them.

'He said Count Agusta had let him have the bikes only on condition that top riders would buy them. The Count didn't want any learners tarnishing his reputation.

'I kept on at Bill and finally he broke; he agreed to lend Mike the single-knocker. I entered him for the Easter Monday meeting at Oulton Park.

'At Oulton Bill and I got our heads together and decided to over-jet and overgear the MV to save wear and tear on the motor—and to slow Mike up a bit. I told Mike to follow Bill round during the race to see how it should be done.

'But when the flag fell Mike was left on the line. He got it going okay—but everybody had cleared off. Mike worked his way through the field. Bill was lying about sixth or seventh, hanging around for Mike and looking over his shoulder to see where he had got to. Within four laps Mike was on his tail. Bill told me later that when Mike caught up he waved him on to pass. He fell in behind Mike to get a closer look at him through Oulton's tricky bits.

'After the race Bill and I had a chat about Mike's possibilities. I was really surprised when he told me that Mike looked all over a champion; I told him he was talking rubbish. But it was food for thought, because Bill was an old hand in the business and knew what he was talking about. He had discovered many, many riders and recommended them to the Count.

'I kept Mike in the smaller classes to start with, on machines he could handle. The 500 cc classes would have been too tough for a beginner and he would most likely have had a series of disappointments.

'I'm sure that if I'd allowed him to enter the bigger classes he would have had enough setbacks to force him out of racing. It was better that he should work his way up, get experience among the lightweights. It paid off. When he eventually moved up to the 500s he was good and ready.'

For a great part of his life Mike has suffered with direct and indirect remarks to the effect that his father has 'bought' success. These rash accusations, usually made by envious riders, anger both Mike and his father. I put this point to them both. Mike flushed and said, 'What a lot of rubbish! My father helped me at the start just as any other would if he was in the same position. It was still me that had to ride the machines—money can't do anything for you when you're on your own dicing with the others. Money can't buy ability.'

Mike's father was a little cooler in his reply. He said quietly, 'I've heard all about this dozens of times. Sure, I helped him in the beginning. But *only* in the beginning. I'm opposed to parents who spoil their children and give them anything they want just because they hold out their hands.'

He nodded across at Mike. 'He doesn't look spoilt, does he? And he bloody well wasn't. If anything I was too hard with him; but only for his own good. He realizes that now.

'My rules in business worked well enough, and I applied precisely the same ones to the business of bringing Mike up. If you want anything badly enough you've got to work for it, sweat for it, strain your back for it. The effort, even if there is help at the start, has to be all your own. That way you get most satisfaction.

'Anything Mike has achieved he has done *largely* as a result of his own talents allied to effort. All he has had out of me from the start has been enthusiasm, encouragement, advice and a temporary loan. He borrowed money to buy his first 125 and he paid it back.

'He won enough money to buy an Itom for ninety pounds, and with the prize-money from this and the 125 he got together enough to buy a 200 cc MV on hire-purchase. During the winter at the end of his season he worked at my showroom in Manchester; he saved the money he earned there and poured it back into his bikes.

'He was in the "red" to me for the first eighteen months of his career. But he was proving something to me: he was prepared to earn his own way. Financial backing from me was there . . . if he needed it. His independence wouldn't allow him to take advantage of it and he struggled through.'

Mike took up the story. 'Stan may have been in great danger of injuring himself falling off his wallet but I couldn't squeeze anything out of him without guaranteeing I would pay him back.

'He's always been a showman, and I suppose that when I first started people were fooled into thinking that he had poured thousands into backing me. One example of his showmanship was when he bought a van for the bikes. Most of the boys were paying around £500 for new light vans to use to transport the machines, but Stan paid £200 for a big second-hand one. Then he had it done up to make it look brand new. He had it painted cream with big red lettering all over it. It was a bit flash, to say the least. It caused a stir and created the idea that we had spent a fortune; but it was a wise, cheap buy. We fitted it out like a mobile workshop. There was room for six bikes, a place for the mechanic and me to sleep. We had a work-bench fitted in it, welding equipment and a vice. Oh, and a wash-basin. It was always Stan's belief that the image of motor-cycle racers had suffered enough, and that I should keep myself clean and tidy. He used to go mad at me for not buying new gear when my leathers and boots became worn. I couldn't afford to buy new leathers; Stan's demands for repayment didn't leave me too much to spare!'

Mike looked across at his father and said, 'The only thing he's given me for free is this nose. I'll never forgive him for that. I look like Mr Punch.'

Completely unconsciously, but almost as if to prove the point, the pair became involved in a bit of tight bargaining.

'Give me a couple of francs for an ice lolly, Mike.'

'I'm not made of money.'

'Oh, come on, I haven't got any with me. I'm sweltering.'

Said Mike, 'I'll tell you what, I'll lend it you.' Then he added, 'I'll lend you enough for three—and you can treat us.'

They both laughed uproariously at the deadly serious business they had just completed, and Stan said, 'See what a businessman he is now.' To me, he added, 'I bet he buys dinner.'

'You'll be lucky,' said Mike.

And they tossed a coin to settle the issue.

At dinner Mike, whose command of French is excellent, guided us through the menu with the expertise and good taste of a man with a wealth of world-wide experience behind him.

He munched his way through his favourite prawn cocktail and listened studiously as his father, with a sure-footed confidence in the infallibility of his own memory, re-ran the events of a decade before.

His references to the early days of Mike's career are liberally sprinkled with the royal plural. Only when he refers to Mike's maturity in motor-cycle racing does he drop the 'we' and substitute 'Mike'. This is not a lapse; it is a simple fact. Mr Hailwood's direct support—though not his enthusiasm—waned when Mike was able to stand on his own two feet. Up until that point they were a racing partnership, father and son, rider and manager. A team.

'When we started winning on the small machines we poured the money right back into the business, into other machinery. Into tuning. Into better equipment. At first we looked after our own bikes. Then, when we'd earned enough to get a stable of three bikes, all of which were earning their keep and ours, we engaged a mechanic. Up to then we had done all our own work on the bikes.

'I reckoned that to put the final gloss and winning streak on the machines we needed an expert tuner. I remembered the man who had tuned my MG for me when I went for the world one-hour record at Brooklands: Bill Lacey. Bill had tuned the MG to a fine edge and I was lapping Brooklands at 114 m.p.h., a staggering speed for those days.

'I went to see him and asked him if he'd tune Mike's machines. He wasn't too happy about the idea. He said he'd lost touch with bikes and hadn't tuned one for twenty-five years. I kept at him, though—I had so much faith in his ability—and told him he'd soon get back into his stride. He was adamant in his refusals, but I knew that if I could only get him back into the atmosphere of the track the smell of oil and octane would do the rest.

'I invited him along to Silverstone to watch Mike test some machines. I think he realized Mike was no mug and this, allied to the atmosphere, sparked off the old feeling for wanting to get to work on motor-bikes again. After watching the way Mike could ride, Bill said he would do his best to help with the tuning. His decision was as much a turning-point in Mike's career as anything; we both valued his assistance. He was the tuner *par excellence* and he fully bore out the faith I had in him. Bikes which had been good were suddenly better under his expert touch.'

In his bid to further Mike's motor-cycle-racing education, Stan Hailwood sent him off to South Africa, with the Manchester rider Dave Chadwick and a mechanic, John Dadley, for company. It was in the winter following Mike's first season.

Mike said, 'That trip to Africa was a real eye-opener. Those riders must have been the hardest cases in the game; if you got in their way it was just too bad, they'd drive straight through you. I found the racing there much tougher than it had been in England, and a good bit wilder. When the flag dropped it was like the Charge of the Light Brigade, but there were some good men, men who were extremely hard to beat.'

The experience honed off many of Mike's rough edges, and, in the face of such determined opposition, instilled in him an even greater will to win and a dedication not to be frightened off by men who were considerably wilder in their style. He returned to England with a mountain of silverware, a trail of broken records, more money than he had taken with him and the South African National Championship, which had fallen to the NSU he had bought from John Surtees. He came back the day before his eighteenth birthday, to find a clamour of people chasing him for interviews, advertising and publicity endorsements, race offers and radio recordings.

He was dubbed 'The Fastest Teenager on Earth' by a newspaper in England, and the cry found echoes all over Europe. The BP group used his name on their advertising and called him 'remarkable'. Alpha Bearings took space in the newspapers and their script described him as 'the amazing teenage motor-cycle racer'. Avon Tyres simply listed his successes.

'I could hardly believe it was all happening to me,' said Mike. 'In one year—between one April and the next—I had become somebody. I was in a whirl. Do you know, I won more races on my first trip to Africa than Geoff Duke had on his trip the year before mine.'

'Aye, and he was a world champion,' said Stan Hailwood, his pride showing.

Mike went on, 'Africa was a terrific experience. Some of the circuits were out in the sticks and just about as primitive as you could see anywhere. The Port Elizabeth 200, for instance, was run in the wilds over a nine-mile circuit that was really rough. There were donkeys and tortoises all over the place. It was a bit hairy.

'When I came back home I jumped in at the deep end straight away. I didn't take any time off and entered for as many races as I could, just as fast as I could write the details on the entry forms. The bug had bitten me good and hard. It must have done—I paid seventy-five pounds excess baggage to bring my NSU engine back with me. I carried it under my arm; I wanted to use it in the very next meeting. It had seen me through twenty races in Africa, and I wanted Bill Lacey to tune it.'

Mike has been back to South Africa every year since 1957, and in 1967 he set up a partnership with the former Suzuki rider Frank Perris in a building business in Durban.

'That first trip wasn't only memorable for the racing. Don't forget I was still a very callow youngster; my eyes were everywhere, I couldn't see enough. Everything was new to me, and I was the typical tourist when I wasn't racing. Dave Chadwick didn't stop at showing me the way round all the circuits; he took me all over the place.

'We went through the game parks to look at the animals; Zulu reservations, waterfalls, the lot. And I did so much walking around the big cities that I'm sure I got to know them as well as the locals. It's so different with me now, I've got blasé about it all. I suppose when you've done as much travelling as I have since those days it's bound to happen.'

Stan told me, 'When Mike and Dave were in Africa I flew out to check up on them. I was horrified to find that Mike had picked up the dreadful habit they had out there of using their feet like speedway riders. So many of them had started in dirt- and grass-track racing that it came natural to them. Mike was very impressionable, and he quickly adopted the habit. When I saw him do it in a race I made him give it up—but not before I'd given him a good telling-off.'

Mike said, 'One habit I didn't pick up—I'm relieved to say—was the local boys' talent for running out of road. They did it with complete abandon—it was second nature to them because there was so much free space around the side of the tracks. I'll bet one or two of them have had a few shocks when they've raced in England or on the Continent.

'Apart from that, though, I was amazed at their ingenuity. Not only were they good riders, but most of them were superb mechanics too. Spares for racing machines were terribly difficult to get hold of, but those boys just got down to it and made their own. If they dropped a valve in they'd simply weld bits on top of the piston and *still* they'd go like blazes.

'They all used to help each other, too, even the keenest rivals. They were always willing to lend each other whatever spares they had. The feeling of friendship was unbelievable. A chap only had to take a gearbox out and within a few minutes anybody who could spare the time would be helping out.

'Jim Redman—I met him there for the first time—bent his bike at one meeting. He asked me if he could borrow the handlebars, footrests and tank from my Norton; I couldn't refuse him. Before I was much

Oulton Park—still riding for the love of the sport, on a 125 cc MV with full 'dustbin' fairing! 1958, his second season.

Production racing in the Thruxton 500-miler.

Above : Getting down to business on the 250 NSU in South Africa.

Top right : In South Africa with Dave Chadwick, far left, and, by his side, the veteran Frank Cope. But who's the other guy?

Right : Grasstracking a Matchless as a keep-fit exercise. Pietermaritzburg, South Africa, 1958.

With Bill Lacey, one of the finest tuners in the business, at the start of the 1958 250 cc TT.

After the race. Mike, 3rd, with (*far left*) Provini, 2nd, and nine times world champion Ubbiali, 1st.

I AM ENTHUSIASTICALLY GLAD FOR VICTORIES OF MIKE WHO ALONE SAVED THIS YEAR THE DUCATI PRESTIGE STOP I AM GRATEFUL TO HIM AND TO YOU DEAR MR HAILWOOD WHO ARE VERY LOVELY AND DO ALL YOUR BEST FOR OUR PRODUCTS STOP HURRAH TO THE CHAMPION OF ENGLAND HURRAH TO YOU AND TO THE DUCATI STOP

And five days later:

VERY WELL DONE MIKE STOP THE DUCATI MECCANICA IS PROUD OF YOUR WONDERFUL VICTORY STOP A CORDIAL HUG TO YOU STOP

Mike rode the Ducatis throughout the British season without once being beaten on them. The delighted Dr Montano, anxious to show his appreciation, had an Italian silversmith fashion a special two-foot-high trophy which he presented to Mike.

It would be too easy to list all of Mike's victories, but it is enough to point out that in 1959, his second full season, he became the first man to win three British championships in one day, he won his first classic, the 125 cc Ulster Grand Prix, was third in the world 125 cc championships, fifth in the 250 and took third place in the 500 cc TT with a 100-m.p.h. lap on a single-cylinder Norton. (He also failed his motor-bike driving-test three times!)

'It's odd looking back on those cuttings and pictures of the early days,' said Mike. 'I find it difficult to appreciate that it was me doing all the things the papers were yelling about. "Wonder Boy" ... "Golden Boy" ... "the Oxford Flyer" ... "Mike the Bike". It's a wonder I could still get my helmet on.

'With an old man like Stan round your neck you don't get time to rest on your laurels or sit back and become conceited. He was *still* pointing out my mistakes, and I was still paying him off. I suppose I was earning around £2,000 a year then.

'The physical change in me during the past ten years is staggering. I've filled out and I have far more strength now, but I've lost enough hair to fill a mattress. Stan's years older than I am and he's got more hair than I have. People will be wondering soon who's the father and who's the son, never mind thinking we're brothers.'

Standing out like a beacon to mark every new breakthrough in Mike's career is the TT. The 1958 TT had established him among the top

British riders, and it was the 1961 meeting that propelled him into the world class.

'That was quite a week,' said Mike with a smile.

'You're not kidding,' said his father; 'I lost my best trilby because of you.'

4 TT Hat-Trick

The legend of Mike Hailwood, like so many other legends before it, was born in the Isle of Man. Once a year he has been as much a part of the folklore, as great a tourist attraction, as the fairies, the witches, the superb scenery and the tailless cats.

Hoteliers like to boast that 'Mike Hailwood Slept Here'. Restaurant-owners point to tables and say, 'He sat there.' Publicans say, 'He came in here for a drink.' Scores of girls are proud to admit that they passed through his life. And there are many more who have offered.

Unlike most legends, this particular one can trace its origins back to a precise date. The date is important because more than 100,000 people had made it the start of their holiday. It was a holiday they will never forget: fathers will tell sons about it and sons will remember that their fathers told them about it and tell their sons in turn.

At the Isle of Man in 1961, Mike wrote his first page of history into the TT record-books. This was the year he became the first man to win three TTs in a week. Only a broken gudgeon-pin, a mere thirteen miles from the finish, frustrated his bid for a clean sweep of all the four solo classes.

Stan Hailwood excitedly sent his new brown trilby spinning into the air to be lost in the crowd as he hurried to hug his son at the end of Friday's Senior TT—the race that completed Mike's history-making hat-trick. Three of the world's toughest races had been won by a twenty-one-year-old, plucked from under the noses of the finest racers in the sport. It was an amazing performance.

Mike's triumph on the single-cylinder 500 cc Norton broke the Italian domination of the Senior event and was the first victory for a British bike in seven years. He was also the first man to average more than 100 m.p.h. on a single-cylinder machine, and nobody else has accomplished that mark since 1961.

Mike, recalling that fabulous week, said, 'So much has happened to me during my career that it's difficult to choose between the highlights. But 1961 does stick out in my mind.

'The main reason is that I went across to the island expecting to win nothing—hoping at the best for a place or two—and then I came away with three winner's trophies. I'd have been content to have won only one, but three . . . well, even now I find it hard to believe.

'I had a lot of luck, I'll be the first to admit it, but I had to put in some damned hard riding as well. I suppose many people would point out that if the leaders hadn't been forced out in the 250 and 500 races I wouldn't have won either of them. And that's true to a certain extent; but the main thing is that I had to be thereabouts when it happened and ready to take my chances.

'Luck is part of the game—after all, I had my share of bad fortune. But for that gudgeon-pin going on my AJS when I was leading by two minutes with only thirteen miles to go I would have scooped all the prizes. You've just got to be philosophical about it, whichever way it happens.

'After the TT I felt that I'd really arrived as a motor-cycle racer. Successes on short circuits were all well and good, but a TT win had been my ambition from the start; it was, and still is, the severest test possible for both man and machine. I came of age on the island in more ways than one.'

To Mike fell the honour of giving the Japanese Honda company its first success in the TT, a race that to them was a proving-ground for their thoroughbred machinery, an advertisement of immeasurable value to their commercial ambitions. Mike guided home a 125 cc Honda in the morning of the first day's racing, then, in the afternoon, repeated the winning performance on a 250/four, giving the established works men, Jim Redman and Tom Phillis, a hiding into the bargain.

Honda's gratitude for the achievements of a privateer on borrowed machines against the works aces fell far short of their anxiety to maintain matters at a strict business level; after the races they presented Stan Hailwood with a bill for £200 for shipping the machines from Japan!

By midweek—and Wednesday's Junior (350 cc) race—the island's population had swollen to record levels, the place was at fever pitch and almost without exception everybody wanted to see Mike rattle up the hat-trick of wins.

'It started off as an unlucky day,' said Mike. 'Of all things to happen, our van ran out of petrol on the way up to the circuit. We were stuck. All the gear, the spares and tools, were in the van and, of course, we couldn't move it. There wasn't a petrol-station in sight. I could have got to the circuit all right, but without the van any last-minute adjustments would have been out.

'A young fellow passing on his motor-bike saw we were in trouble and siphoned off all the fuel from his tank into the van. He refused to give us his name or even accept any payment from us.

'When the race started, Gary Hocking, on an MV, steamed away and stayed in front until he had trouble. I took over and with only a couple of laps left I had stretched out a fairly comfortable lead. Just when I thought it was in the bag the gudgeon-pin—of all things—played up and put me out of the race. I had a two-minute lead with only thirteen miles to go.

'All the way back on that last lap people were waving and cheering me. Then, at Milntown, I had to drop out. I watched Phil Read go by on his Norton to win his first TT. Gary Hocking, going like crazy, was the next. He finished second. All I got was a lot of sympathy. I could have wept. But it taught me that luck breaks both ways.'

Mike's performances in those two days of racing turned him into a subject of curiosity; he felt, for the first time, the full, unnerving blast of the public stare. Everywhere he went people wanted to slap his back, shake his hand, speak to him or simply gape. Far from revelling in the adoration, he found it an acute embarrassment, and it eventually reached the stage where he was unwilling to leave the shelter of his hotel. He was a reluctant idol, unconsciously manufacturing his own publicity. . . .

Public-schoolboy. Millionaire's son. Fair-haired and blue-eyed. And, above all, getting to the top in a sport that seemed the most improbable of all professions for a boy of his background. He was, in everything but skill, a square peg in a round hole.

Sitting in his flat, a glass of vodka and lemonade on the table in front of him, Mike swivelled round on the comfortable leather chair and pointed a finger at the TT winner's sashes stretched across the wall.

'See the one third from the top? The Senior '61. That's the one I really wanted, but I never dreamed I'd get it that year. There was so much to beat.

'The Norton I rode—I'll never forget it, it was Number 3—was a piecemeal job fitted together by Bill Lacey. He did a marvellous job on it; he was a genius. He got odd bits and pieces from Lord knows where. There was a 1958 cylinder-head and cambox but new flywheels and crankcase, the old one was split. He shortened the cam drive to suit a 1961 cylinder-barrel and piston. He increased the skirt of the piston clearances by two or three thou, anticipating higher running temperatures with the short, two-ring lay-out. It had twin plugs, an Alpha big-end bearing and flanged drive-side main-bearing housing, and when it was all bench-tested the engine was giving us a fraction over 53 b.h.p.

'Bill's knowledge and experience of gearing and carburetion far surpassed those of any of his contemporaries. I knew that when I sat on a bike that he'd been working on it would be perfectly okay.

'Over breakfast on the morning of the Senior, Stan and I talked over the best method we could use to counteract the advantage of Gary Hocking's big MV. We realized that my Norton couldn't hope to match the MV for speed—there was about ten miles an hour difference.

'We agreed the best plan was for me to stay as near as possible to Gary and pick up some extra time by slip-streaming whenever possible. The theory was good, but in practice it didn't work out like that. When I tried to get near him Gary merely screwed it on a bit and the MVs superior acceleration wafted away any chance I had of hanging on to his tail.

'Yet in the end the plan did work, though not in the way we'd expected. Gary piled on the pressure—and paid the penalty for doing it. He vanished up the slip road at Ballacraine when he hit the bend too fast. I dodged in front, but not for long. He came back like the wind. After that I hung on like a leech. He had trouble, first with the fairing then with plugs, and I picked up some valuable time when he had to pull into the pits for help.

'After that it was plain sailing and the Norton headed for home without even the faintest sign of trouble. Nobody was more surprised than me when I found after the race that I'd averaged more than a hundred, the first time it had been done by a British bike.

'I'd thought it was going to be a slow day; the wind was really blustery. Trying to match Gary's pace upped my times without my realizing it. At the finish I was almost two minutes ahead of Bob McIntyre.

'When we totted up my speeds from the leader-board at the grandstand, I did a double-take at the paint marks that showed the third-lap times. I'd done 101·31 m.p.h.; it just went to show how fast Nortons could be moved. Mine had handled like a dream, and had Bill Lacey's guarantee of reliability stamped all over it.

'When I watched a filmed re-run of the race—it was shot from a helicopter—I was amazed to see how close I had kept to the MV. Every time we went through the tricky bits of the course the gap seemed to narrow. I was obviously picking up a lot of time on the bends then having it pegged back when the MV motored along the straights.'

Underneath Stan Hailwood's veneer of pride at Mike's historic success was the knowledge that some people refused steadfastly to be budged from the view it had been *bought* along with the superior machinery, and that this, as much as anything, ensured victory. They were, of course, quite wrong, but it was not enough for Stan to know that: he had to show them. So before he left the Isle of Man he arranged to buy an AJS which had finished unspectacularly down the field in the 350 race. It was taken to Scarborough, where only the jets and bearing were altered to suit the undulating circuit. Mike won on it, in the rain, in record time. . . .

If Mike's skill was in getting results from whatever machine was put underneath him, his father's was in persuading people to part with the equipment. In this activity he was inexhaustible; he applied his business techniques to the sport.

Curiously, if Mike has a failing it is his complete lack of this business acumen. In short, he cannot be bothered to argue terms or battle out the details. Usually at the first sign of a stumbling-block he gives in. He would rather leave any negotiations to somebody else; bartering embarrasses him. This is why the combination of his talent and his father's incisive business brain have been the perfect alliance. This combination is probably the true reason for the envy shown by others who had neither of the essential components.

Stan Hailwood's gritty determination shows itself in a vastly different way from that demonstrated by Mike. With Mike it stops short at business; with Stan that is where it starts.

Mike explained: 'If you short-changed him a penny he'd be down on you like a ton of bricks. If something is set in his mind it's a devil of a job to shake him off it. Honda had a taste of this at the 1961 TT.

'They'd promised to let us have a 125 and a 250, but they found themselves short of 125s. It looked as if I wasn't going to get one after all; I was quite resigned to it, but Stan wouldn't give up. He almost lived at the Honda camp. They couldn't get rid of him; he was round there morning, noon and night pestering them for a 125. It really looked as if there was no chance when it got to the day before the final practice session, but the old man still wouldn't give in, he kept on at them.

'Finally—I'm sure it was just to get rid of him—they said we could have Luigi Taveri's practice bike. They told us it was a bit the worse for wear, and they weren't joking. Before they could change their minds Stan had it in our van and was back to the hotel like a shot.

'I took it for a spin up the road and it was terrible, it was clapped out. But when we decided to do a practice lap on it I was staggered at the performance, even if it was a well-worn old thing. I told the old man that if it had been on good form I reckon I might have stood a chance in the race. Our mechanics got to work on it, racing against the clock, and they managed to smooth it out a bit. They tightened just about everything they could lay a spanner on. The big question was whether it would last the race. Well, it did, and I won.

'The 250s that year had serious overheating problems and the oil turned as thin as water. After the practice outings the Honda mechanics used to poke a thermometer into the oil-tank, then stand back and watch the mercury shooting sky high. They were obviously worried; perhaps not quite as much as the riders, whose marital ambitions were likely to be fried out of existence.

'We decided to cut an air-vent in the fairing underneath the crank-case. Stan had noticed the air-vents cut into the wings of the Viscount aircraft and reckoned Vickers knew their business, so he copied the *T*-shaped cut. He ignored the idea of a scoop.

'The brainwave seemed to work fine because it certainly kept the engine much cooler. Bob McIntyre, ironically, had to drop out with oil trouble when he was leading. Luck or good planning?'

The planning did not stop there. 'Stan spent thirty pounds having a telephone system put in so that he could keep check on my progress at vital points of the course. The information was phoned back to him at the grandstand, where he was able to work out precisely where I was in relation to the opposition. I must have been the best-informed rider in the races; I knew exactly what I had to do and what was expected of me.

'I suspected then that the old man knocked a few seconds off my lead to keep me on my toes. I preferred, and still do, to have the correct and exact information. The psychology bit is not for me. It's common practice, I know, for people in pits to hang out inaccurate signals. Sometimes it could be a good move, but imagine if you've been going flat out, riding beyond yourself and confident you're streaking away from the rest, and then somebody at the pits sticks the blackboard out and tells you that you're only a few seconds up. You know you've gone over the limit, but according to the signals it's made little impression.

Now, messages like that could make one or two things happen. Either you're likely to write yourself off by trying harder, or you're going to say, "What's the use trying if I can't get away from the others?" and give up.

'The odd thing about the '61 TT was that I wasn't at all tired by the time it was all over. I suppose the elation of winning three out of four glossed over any weariness.

'I was fairly keyed up all week, and with so much going on I didn't get much chance to relax. Just the fact that I was riding such a wide variety of bikes presented enough problems to keep me on my toes. When you compete in only one or two classes, as most riders do, it's easy to remember which gear you should be in for which corner, even if there are about two or three hundred bends in a TT lap. But when you're entered for four races, with gear-boxes ranging from four to seven speeds, it takes a bit of sorting out. You arrive at a corner juggling frantically through the box trying to find one that will get you round all right. More often than not you're left undecided and have to fumble your way along. Somebody once asked me how many gears there were on the 250 Honda. I said I'd only found seven, and I was being honest: I couldn't remember how many there were. Anyway, the seventh was plenty fast enough for me. I wasn't too anxious to find another, it must be murder riding the 50 cc bikes with upwards of twelve speeds to play about with. It's like a lucky dip.

'I decided after that TT to pack up racing the 125s. I felt I was getting too large for them. I was five foot ten, and weighed in at around eleven stone, and it was a hell of a job trying to squeeze myself to half-size in order to get on them. It must have taken some steam out of them to have me aboard. Anyway, they weren't fast enough for my liking. I preferred the 250 Honda; it had terrific pace, but even then it handled dreadfully.

'We kept it for the remainder of 1961. Stan managed it on some sort of fiddle. He told Honda that if they'd let us have a bike he would sell their machinery in Britain; he said he would take on the Honda agency and, as his was the biggest firm in the country, it was a valuable help to them. They needed all the sales they could get just then. And so we had the use of one of the best bikes in the business.

'I wasn't a works rider—it was hard to get a place as a teamster. Jim Redman and Tom Phillis saw to that; they had been in from the start and, naturally, wanted to keep everybody else out. After all, they'd ridden the bikes when they'd been bad, and, obviously, now the machines were good they didn't want anybody else moving in. On top of this I'd already signed a contract to race on Shell and Honda had given their name to Castrol.

'Honda, with their eye on the best British riders, also loaned bikes to John Hartle and Bob McIntyre. But, towards the end of the season, the works bikes were getting better and better and ours were at a standstill, by now fairly well worn and certainly not the threat they had been.

'It must have been a horrible embarrassment to them when I clinched the World Championship in Sweden; but I was lucky. Jim Redman needed to win there—it was the one race that counted—and he fell off.

'Lucky or not, I'd won a world title, and that's all I was interested in. It was bad luck for Jim, but it would have been worse if it had happened to me.

'It was round about this time that everything seemed to happen with bewildering speed. I hardly had time to catch a breath.

'Before I went to Sweden for the last race in the championship series Count Agusta had watched me, after being told all about me by Bill Webster, the MV distributor in England. He said he had enjoyed my riding. And then he didn't *ask* me to join MV: he told me to. It was as simple as that. I was flabbergasted. There was no attempt to persuade me it was best for my career, no haggling or arguing over terms. There was such a long queue of riders just waiting for the opportunity to climb on an MV that you didn't think twice about offers like that. And, of course, I accepted.

'At Monza, in the last-but-one grand prix in the series, I rode both MVs, the 350 and the 500, and the 250 Honda. The MVs were my first outings on full-blown works bikes, and I won the 500 and was second to Gary Hocking in the 350. I was over the moon.

'The year had been good, what with three TTs, a world title against the works men and, to top it all, a contract that would give me the chance to ride the best bikes in the world.

'I don't know whether it went to my head, but I went wild and broke out into a rash of high living. I had a new-found freedom because I was no longer under Stan's direct control. I took a flat with a few other blokes and we lived it up to no mean tune. Too many women, I think, popped into and out of my life with what became almost boring frequency. I drank too much and went to far too many all-night parties. I lost a hell of a lot of sleep and with it that vital fine edge of fitness. That flat was like a madhouse, a death-trap for a man in my profession.

'The result was that, living as I did throughout that winter, I started the 1962 season an extremely tired man. On top of that I was faced with the problems of adapting myself to the intricacies of riding four-cylinder MVs, whereas all my experience on big bikes had been with the uncomplicated singles in the 500 and 350 classes.

'If that wasn't enough, 1962 was a year when a lot of good blokes, riders who really knew the business, were getting killed. Losing friends in crashes I had seen upset me badly, and this, along with all the other trouble I'd brought upon myself, affected my riding. I would say that 1962 was the year when my riding was at its worst; all in all, it's a year I would prefer to forget.

'Tom Phillis was killed trying to keep up with Gary Hocking and me in the Junior TT. His Honda was underpowered and handled badly, and what he lost in speed he tried to make up with sheer riding skill and daring. Tom's death upset Gary so much that he decided to retire from motor-bike racing. He was inconsolable. He cleared off back home to Rhodesia to try and forget. Then he made up his mind to try his hand at car racing, and he was killed practising for a race. It was grimly ironic that having quit bike racing because it was getting far too dangerous he should be killed in a racing car.

'Jim Redman was awfully upset. It was bad enough when Tom died but when Gary went as well that was almost too much for him; he made up his mind to give it up, then later changed his mind. For my part, I was shaken, but I worked it out that there was no escaping the fact that if you go racing there are risks to be considered. If you spend time worrying about spills you're not going to get very far; you have to put any thoughts like that clean out of your mind. You live with that narrow margin between life and death all the time, and any additional worrying is not going to help concentration.

'How much it affects you when somebody is killed obviously depends a lot on how well you know him. If it's a stranger, then, obviously, it doesn't mean very much. It's like reading in the paper that someone you've never heard of has been knocked down by a bus. If it's a friend, then of course you feel it more; but you can't afford to show it. You simply have to get on with the job or pack it up all together. It's no good going on racing and thinking all the time that "old so and so was killed doing what I'm doing now".

'Oddly enough, you can fall off a bike at a hundred miles an hour and often come out of it with fewer injuries than the chap who crashes his family car at fifteen.'

Mike fingered his Corsican-bandit-type moustache, camouflage for a scar he suffered in a car crash after the Race of the Year at Mallory Park in 1967.

'My worst fear isn't so much being killed as being badly injured and having stitches; the thought of that gives me goose-pimples. Whenever I fall off, the first thing I do when my head stops spinning is to give myself an examination. I gingerly prod round as many parts as I can comfortably reach, and I think, "Oh God, don't let there be anything wrong that might need stitching up."

'After the spills I have had I've been terrified to look under my leathers in case there's something wrong that isn't actually hurting. I remember falling off at Brands Hatch once, and getting up off the ground to see blood pouring from one of my gloves. I thought I'd lost a finger, I was bleeding so much, but I couldn't bring myself to look. I stood there like an idiot, staring at the mess and thinking, of all things, that my piano-playing would be ruined. When I eventually plucked up sufficient courage to take a look, I was astonished to see that when I waggled my fingers they all waggled back. Ten of them. All I had was a tiny cut on one of them which was bleeding profusely. By the time help arrived I'd gathered together what was left of my public image and I managed to say, in what I imagined was a nonchalant manner, "Oh, it's nothing. Nothing to worry about. . . ." If I'd thought it was to be a stitching job I'm sure they'd have found me in a dead faint.

'Jim Redman's particular fear was losing his teeth. Wherever he landed, as soon as he'd confirmed he was alive, he used to prod about in his mouth to make sure all his teeth were in place. Then he did what most of us do first, a quick check around the lower reaches. I think he had his priorities wrong somewhere. Having your teeth knocked out doesn't stop you eating. . . .'

5 MV

When the big jets dip their noses through the haze that seems to persist around Northern Italy and head towards Malpensa Airport, one of the two that serve Milan, you can gaze out of the windows at one of the district's most famous landmarks. Its roofs shimmer through a wood that skirts the airport perimeter. Guards, protecting its secrets, patrol the area. It is the MV factory—Meccanico Verghera.

Verghera is the village nearest Malpensa Airport. Count Dominico Agusta owns a large slice of the village, as well as the land on which the airport has been built. Monza, the scene of many of his successes, lies about forty miles away, Modena about a hundred.

Count Agusta is to motor-cycles what Enzo Ferrari is to cars; they are two tycoons whose names and products have earned world-wide fame. Two Italians who have only to snap their fingers for the cream of riders and drivers to rush to sign contracts to represent their factories.

Over the years the planes that have swept into Malpensa have carried some of the most famous names in motor-cycle racing: Les Graham, Gary Hocking, John Surtees, John Hartle, Alan Shepherd, Bill Lomas, Tarquinio Provini, Carlo Ubbiali, Giacomo Agostini, Mike Hailwood.

Each one has found a good deal of fame, earned the wholehearted envy of those other riders who weren't chosen, and, at the same time, amassed large amounts of money for his efforts. There is not a rider in the game who wouldn't sign to ride the Count's thoroughbred machinery.

The trophy-room at the MV factory bears its own testimony to the reliability, smoothness and power of the Count's motor-bikes. The room is a splash of silver—walls lined with cups, shields and trophies from races all over the globe.

There have been faster bikes than the MV, but there have been no better ones. Their reliability has been consistent, so much so that a breakdown is treated with incredulous disbelief by the Press and with biting self-examination by the MV mechanics.

In the sprawl of buildings that house Count Agusta's empire of racing perfection, one-third is given over to the development of his motor-cycles. The remainder is used for the building of helicopters, his main business.

Mike talks about the Count with a mixture of reverence and reserve. His four years at MV brought him a wide range of troubles and triumphs; he left at the end of that time knowing little more about his enigmatic employer than he had when he first joined the factory.

'Almost his whole life revolves around his business,' said Mike. 'He's thrown himself into it with typical Italian thoroughness. He is the iron-handed, autocratic boss who never leaves to somebody else what he can do himself. There are no directors at MV, only varying levels of employment. There is no doubt in anybody's mind that the Count is Number One, and he makes certain they don't forget it.

'It would be difficult to get five shillings out of the factory without his personal endorsement. He has his finger firmly on the pulse: nothing happens there that he doesn't know about. Every action, every move through the works has to have his personal signature before it is approved and accepted. Nobody dares make a decision without first consulting him—Lord help them if they did. I think they're all terrified of him and the power he wields.

'This is probably a fine, workable set-up for the efficiency of the factory and the business, but it was no good to me. I could never keep out of his way as his minions did, and it caused one or two differences between us. I was just as stubborn as he was, and situations developed where we just stood and faced each other like a couple of bulls, neither one prepared to give way.

'For instance, he was so busy keeping tabs on everything that his appointments used to pile up in great heaps as the day went on. Because he refused to delegate any responsibility he always fell far behind the clock. This annoyed me beyond all measure. Time after time I've been to the factory, probably having flown all the way from England, only to be kept waiting for hours on end.

'I remember he fixed an appointment once for me to see him. I was at the factory dead on time, but it was *three days* before I got in to meet him. I hung around the place for a few hours each day until I became so angry that I told his secretary to inform him that so far as I was concerned he could drop dead, and I stormed out of the place. I knew he'd

At the Ulster Grand Prix, 1959, with East German ace Ernst Degner and the late Gary Hocking.

Aboard the Desmo 125 Ducati in practice for the 1959 TT on the Clypse circuit.

The innards of the 250 Ducati.

Mike, third on a Norton in the 1960 Senior TT, in the winner's enclosure with (*far left*) John Hartle, who was second, and John Surtees, who won.

Mike, tracked by Swiss ace Luigi Taveri, steers a Honda to a first Japanese TT victory in the 1961 Lightweight race.

been in his office all the time because people who had come to see him after he went in ahead of me.

'The fact that he was the one who had arranged the appointment and fixed the time didn't help my temper. It was maddening to be kept waiting so long, and I couldn't hide my anger any longer. I was already in my car and heading back to my hotel when I looked in the mirror and saw a fleet of his workers pedalling after me on push-bikes, shouting, "Come back, Mister Mike, come back." It looked as if their lives depended on it; and, when I think about it, that was probably just what it amounted to.

'I swallowed my pride and went back with them, but I was still kept waiting until he was quite ready to see me. I'm convinced that he was trying to establish some sort of psychological superiority over me, showing me who was the boss. His men were horrified by my attitude but I was determined not to give in.

'Every move he made—everything about MV, in fact—seemed to be designed to give him this psychological advantage. It was really important to him to show that he was the boss.

'When you drive along the wooded lane that leads to the factory, past the armed guards and the dogs, you arrive at his outer office. It's like a post-office counter. There's a receptionist's window with a speak-through hole in the glass. You say who you are, what your business is, then wait for the summons from the inner sanctum.

'The first thing that hits when you eventually walk into the Count's office is an impressive array of trophies. Then you turn to the right and there he is: Count Agusta. He normally wears a grey suit and sits at a desk built onto a dais, some eighteen inches above the floor. He motions you to sit in the chair in front of the desk, so that he's looking down at you. . . .

'He professes not to speak English, although I have since been told that he does. He usually had an interpreter with him at our meetings, but sometimes I had to struggle and stumble along in Italian; he spoke back so fast that I found it difficult to grasp the flow of the conversation. He has a typical tycoon's way of talking, staccato and businesslike. He doesn't waste words. Once he gives an order, that's that; there's no arguing against his decisions.

'I caught him off guard at one appointment. I was waiting in his secretary's office to see him when he did something that was unheard of—he came out of his office to see me. I couldn't believe it. He sat in his secretary's chair, and I moved to sit on the edge of the desk so that

I was looking down on him, a reversal of his usual advantage. He didn't like this change in our situations at all, and he shot out of the chair, beckoning me to follow him back into his office. Once he was there he stepped up onto the dais, sat himself down behind his big oak desk and looked down on me. We were back to normal.

'He only has to ask one of his men to come to his office to have them quaking in their boots wondering what's wrong. They always assume something is—a summons from the Count isn't often the prelude to good news. No matter how long they're with him, they have to stand while he does all the talking. He's only five-foot-five tall, but he commands enormous respect; his workers stand awe-struck and silent in his presence unless he asks them a question.

'Because of the long hours he works—he starts about ten-thirty in the morning and carries on right through until two or three the following morning, except for a couple of hours for lunch—it's not unusual to be called before him as late as ten at night.

'He has geared everything for ease of movement in the smooth running of his businesses. He has a villa in the grounds of the factory, two minutes' walk from his office. He also has an apartment in Milan. He has a swivel chair at his desk so that he can spin round to get at the radio-telephone link he has with his helicopters, or to slide over to the battery of telephones that never seem to stop ringing.

'I got a call from him once at my hotel inviting me to dinner at the villa. He asked me to take one of my mechanics along. The poor fellow was almost a nervous wreck. He was shaking like a leaf, wondering what he had done wrong. He couldn't believe that he had been invited for anything as harmless as a pleasant dinner and a bit of conversation. He imagined he was for the high jump, though however he racked his memory he couldn't think what he might have done wrong. He didn't relax until we were clear of the villa.

'I learnt what all the panic was about when I felt the full blast of the Count's anger early in 1964, and we had the mother and father of arguments.

'There was a meeting at Imola. Geoff Duke had got the Gileras out of retirement and he'd picked John Hartle and Derek Minter to ride them. It was a race that the Italians had waited a long time to see: Gileras versus MVs in Italy. There was going to be no room to spare among the spectators at Imola.

'My start-money was terrific—around £1,000, I think. Then, before the Italian race, I went to Brands Hatch and crashed. I hurt my wrist but I decided the money offered at Imola was too good to miss. I fancied the idea of having a go at the Gileras, too.

'It was an unwise decision. I shouldn't even have thought about racing, especially against men like Hartle and Minter on Gileras. My wrist hadn't fully mended; it was still sore and not very strong. I'd only covered two or three laps when the wrist started giving me hell. I led the Gileras for about ten laps, but then the wrist gave way completely. John and Derek breezed by and left me in third place, and even then I didn't have the sense to pack up.

'The Count, as usual, didn't come to the circuit to spectate; he stayed at the villa, watching the race on television. It must have been embarrassing for him to sit and watch the MV, his pride and joy, being whacked by his biggest rival factory.

'He had me in his office the following morning, and for once I wasn't kept waiting. He laid into me as hard as he knew how; he told me I'd ridden like an old woman and shamed the good name of the MV. He said I should have stopped rather than be beaten. I couldn't help myself; I yelled back at him just as loudly. I told him that if he thought he could do any better he should ride the bloody thing himself. At that I strode out, leaving him flabbergasted at my outburst. The mechanics were terrified—they could see their jobs flying out of the window.

'But the row seemed to clear the air. After I'd been back at the hotel an hour the Count called me and invited me back to his office. We had a chat, and he was full of charm and apologies—and apologies from him were rare.

'He has a great way of ending interviews; he leaves you in no doubt that they're over and done with. When he's finished saying his piece he steps down from his dais and almost lifts you out of the seat by shaking your hand and hauling on it at the same time. Then, with one hand firmly around your shoulder, he steers you to the door and out through it.

'It's difficult to predict his moods, but when he's in an expansive and kindly mood he can be the epitome of charm. I remember, for instance, an occasion in 1965 when I was flying off to the Argentine Grand Prix and had to break the journey in Italy. I landed at Linate and had to get to Malpensa, about forty miles away, for the connection. It meant a long journey by coach or taxi and a four-hour wait for the flight.

'When I flew into Linate there was a chauffeur-driven car supplied by the Count waiting for me at the airport. It whisked Stan and me off to the MV factory, where the Count had laid on a champagne snack; it was ten o'clock at night but he was still there working. He had a contract ready that he wanted me to sign for the following season. He dictated the terms, which were extremely generous, and added that he was insuring me for £10,000. An hour and a half later he had put us back in the car and we were off, business finished, to the airport. It was there, I suppose, that I finally made up my mind not to switch over completely to cars.

'Somehow the Count had found out that I was on that particular aircraft and was making sure he got hold of me to sign the contract. It was a pleasant surprise to me. I had grown used to his offhand attitude, and now I was seeing the other side of him.

'He is only so much of a mystery to people in the motor-cycle business because that is the way he has organized his life. For a man so avidly interested in the sport he watches very little of it live. He seems to thrive on reading the result-sheets rather than seeing how they're compiled. Maybe another reason he doesn't go to many meetings is because he doesn't like flying. He prefers to travel around on his big yacht or in his private train. On the shorter journeys his chauffeur drives him in one of the half a dozen cars he always has standing by, maybe the Ferrari or the Cadillac. He has his yacht moored at Naples. He used to offer me cruises on it around the Adriatic or the Mediterranean, but I never went. I didn't fancy sailing round with people I didn't know: that's my anti-social streak coming out.

'Almost all the time he can spare from running his helicopter business—it's tied in with the Bell company of America—is devoted to his hobby, producing superb racing bikes. They are his pets.

'His big ambition was always to see a home-grown rider take the MVs to the top of the world championships. But really good Italian riders have been a little scarce in recent years, so he's had to sign foreigners. I won four world titles for him in successive years and took the TT three times on the run.

'But, as I say, over the years he'd been on the look-out for an Italian to do it. In 1965 he found one in Agostini, a truly great rider who's finally fulfilled all the Count's ambitions by twice winning the world 500 cc championship.

'Agostini, who comes from Bergamo, was riding for Morini when the Count heard of him and recognized his talents. Ago didn't have too many races outside Italy but on home ground he was terrific, and the Count invited him to join the team.

'For my money, Agostini is the finest Italian rider since Ubbiali; he's a quick learner, he has plenty of courage and he's brimming with skill. After I left MV for Honda he gave me the hardest rides I'd ever experienced, not only on the 500 but on the 350 as well.

'When he joined MV and he was in the running for the Italian Championship the Count asked me to let Agostini win at Riccione and San Remo; he told me to take second place. I was annoyed because I reckoned he should have to beat me on his own merits and not be given anything if he was to prove himself. I had far more to lose than he had and I was certainly going to give nothing away.

'In the event, I had to try really hard to get the better of him; I was surprised to find that he was so good. As it turned out he did win both the races, so all my anger at being told to back down was wasted. In the first race I had braking trouble, then, at the other, a mysterious ailment developed and I had to pull out.

'It was my resolve, however, that if Agostini was going to achieve world-championship status, even if we were in the same team, he would have to beat me to do it.

'I was the number-one rider for MV according to my contract, and naturally I had the choice of the best bikes for both the 350 and 500 cc events. But in 1965, when Jim Redman took a tumble at the Nürburgring and Agostini got a third place at the TT after I'd been forced out with mechanical trouble, Count Agusta saw his chance to give Agostini a title. He decided that Agostini should go ahead for the world 350 championship and he issued instructions that the best 350s should be given to him. Agostini stood a good chance of winning the title at the Japanese Grand Prix. I was put in the unenviable position of holding off Jim Redman to let Agostini get ahead to win the race and the championship.

It was a particularly unenviable job because I had just agreed to join Honda, and this was to be my last ride for MV, but my loyalty to MV and Agostini had to take first place and I know that Jim realized my spoiling tactics couldn't be avoided.

As it turned out, Agostini broke down when he was leading. I moved into first place and Jim was second – but clearly the Count had found his man, an Italian brilliant enough to fulfil his nationalistic ambitions. Agostini certainly hasn't let him down, and the Count must have been overjoyed when his home-bred rider became the first Italian to clinch a "double" during the 1968 TT.

'The Count was a terribly difficult man to understand; I could never fathom him. As I said, at one and the same time he could be the most charming and the most irritating man one ever met. But there is no escaping the fact that he makes the best racing bikes in the world. If I had the choice I'd always ride the big MV 500 in the TT. It's perfect for the job.'

6 One Day's Work

He sat Buddha-fashion, legs crossed under him, gnawing absent-mindedly at each finger cuticle until it bled. He stopped only to yawn and stretch frequently as all men do when their nerves are being taxed. He couldn't bite his nails, because he had already sheared them down with his teeth.

His reflection in the mirror at the foot of the bed returned his critical stare. It showed a receding hairline and a strangely mature face for a man twenty-seven years of age.

'Look at me, I look a hundred years old. An old man before my time. That's what racing does to you,' said Mike. His edginess overshadowed his usual carefree outlook; he was forcing himself into the shell out of which he would spring in a couple of hours' time. It was the morning of the 1967 Senior TT. At 1.30 that June afternoon he was scheduled to meet his greatest rival, Giacomo Agostini, in a bid to clinch his 12th TT and keep his world-championship hopes alive.

The responsibility of the race, which was to be watched by 100,000 people, weighed heavily on his shoulders. Agostini, brilliant and daring, had the 500 cc MV Agusta, a machine that was slower than Mike's Honda but handled perfectly. The Honda's almost uncontrollable instability, even on the straights, was Mike's main worry.

The build-up to Mike's tension had started the night before. It doesn't show outwardly until he begins his ritual of nail-biting, and even then it isn't immediately obvious. But on that night before the race it had broken through sharply in a moment of irritation.

Mike and I were having dinner at the Casino when he noticed a man at an adjoining table staring hard at him. Every time Mike looked up the man's unblinking gaze met him, until he could take it no longer; rudeness had gone beyond the bounds of curiosity. It made Mike uncomfortable. He leant towards the man's table and said angrily, 'I'm not in a bloody zoo, you haven't paid to gawp at me.' The hint was taken—as it could scarcely fail to be—and the man began to pay more attention to his Lobster Thermidor, which would undoubtedly have finished up on his head had he carried on his unnerving rudeness.

With that off his chest, Mike, acutely aware now of the crushing tension, began to look for some way of staving it off for a while. He went into the Casino's gaming-room and cheerfully gambled away about £50 of the £400 he had won a couple of nights earlier on the blackjack table. He stopped when a crowd began to form around his shoulders and escaped to the solitude of his third-floor room.

The hotel manager, Mr Alex O'Brien, alert to the whims and vagaries of champions, had arranged for Mike to have a three-roomed suite in the quietest corner of the sea-front Casino Hotel. It was far-sighted wisdom on the part of a man who had once trained professional boxers and understood the problems of tension.

Before he went off to bed, Mike told me, 'I don't feel like being alone in the morning; pop up and see me about ten o'clock. We'll have some breakfast in my room.' As I left he was hooking a *Do Not Disturb* notice on the door-handle.

Mike doesn't sleep well; his night is broken up into a series of something like ten catnaps. In between these he reads avidly until he falls asleep again, or searches the waveband of his powerful portable radio looking for music programmes. The radio and stacks of books and magazines are the first items to be packed into his luggage when he goes away from home. He told me, 'I have a dreadful time trying to sleep through the night. Not only when I'm racing, but out of season too. And I'm terrified of taking sleeping tablets. I don't want to get hooked on those things.'

In the morning I met his father in the hotel foyer. He looked anxiously at his watch, which was showing 10.30 a.m., and asked me, 'Is Mike up yet?'

'No.'

'Hadn't you better give him a shout?'

'Why don't you wake him up?' I said. 'I'll be up in a few minutes.'

His answer surprised me. 'No thank you! I daren't go anywhere near him before a race. I'll leave it to you.'

It was a sleepy voice that answered my knock, but the sleepiness vanished with startling suddenness. When he wakes Mike is immediately alive, clear-eyed and bright, showing no traces of a restless night. He ordered his usual hotel breakfast of two chicken sandwiches and tea—not coffee, which he doesn't like. Inevitably he switched on the radio, filling the room with pop songs. The chambermaid, aloof and businesslike, put the tray of sandwiches on the dressing-table then blushed pink as Mike teased, 'Are you going to nip into bed for a while?'

He roared as she replied, 'I haven't got time . . . no . . . oh, Lord . . . I didn't mean it that way. You are cheeky, Mr Hailwood. Anyway, you'd be better off eating your sandwiches.'

Outside the sun was blazing in a cloudless sky, but the beach was deserted. The sun was no match as a tourist attraction for the racing, and the thousands of people who could have been tanning themselves were already making their way to the circuit.

Like jugglers warming the audience for the main attraction, the 50 cc men were racing round the circuit, dexterously working their twelve gears on a three-lap race that acted more as a filler to the morning than a spectacle. They were already getting rid of their own tensions. Mike was waiting nervously for the chance to escape from his—it couldn't come quickly enough for him.

The agonies of pre-race nerves torture Mike's stomach almost to the limit of its endurance. Those proverbial butterflies suggest only a gentle fluttering, almost a pleasant tremor, but the true feeling is something a great deal more violent and unenjoyable. Generally it isn't fear, though in some cases it could be; more often it is acute apprehension, a keying-up process where the nerves are drawn tighter and tighter.

To people who do not race, or who have no contact with racing or any competition of similar nature, it must be difficult to appreciate this draining process that can leave a man limp. But everybody knows the feeling, the awful inevitability, of a visit to the dentist. The symptoms are similar, and the quite unreasonable elation afterwards again parallels that of a racer, another personal triumph over doubt.

The fact that he could be leaving the circuit in an ambulance doesn't worry Mike nearly so much as the dread that he may be leaving it without the victor's laurel over his shoulders.

The two fears are not as contradictory as many people might imagine. The worry for a champion like Mike revolves not around whether he will emerge from the fray without physical injury—he is completely confident in his ability to do that—but around whether he will emerge without damage to the reputation he guards so fiercely and jealously.

The apprehension increases steadily as the time for the race draws nearer. It is outwardly apparent in his constant yawning and frequent visits to the lavatory; inwardly, in his churning stomach, prickling skin and anxiety to get under way.

To say he has *never* been afraid for his neck would be to stretch his reputation for apparent nervelessness to ridiculous lengths. He has, and he is not ashamed to admit it. Almost in the same breath, however, he says those moments have, mercifully, been few and far between.

The weight of responsibility to employers who have paid him small fortunes to race their machinery is another worry which is very much in his thoughts. His professional pride and thoroughness, his determination to earn his money, leave him absolutely no margin for careless relaxation when he is working. He realizes, in any case, that no champion can ever afford to give anything less than his best. One international rider once told me, 'I know Hailwood is the top-paid man in the business, and I might be short of cash from time to time, but I wouldn't like to be in his shoes. He's just *got* to be on form all the time. I prefer to stay poor and do without the ulcers.'

Mike looked thoughtfully from the balcony outside his room across the wide sweep of the horseshoe-shaped beach and bay. He was staring towards the hotel where Agostini and the MV men were staying. They call the hotel 'Casa Agostini', because of the stream of telephone calls he gets from admiring girls who phone just to talk to him or to make more blatant offers. Agostini is gay and good-looking, with that flair for speed that seems to be born to all Italians. The wall around the phone is a graffiti telephone directory of girls he must 'phone urgently'. Mike had stayed at 'Casa Agostini' when he was riding for MV. Now he had changed camps—and hotels.

He turned from the balcony, checked the time on his wristwatch, and nodded towards the hotel across the bay. 'I wonder what he's feeling like. He can't be feeling half as bad as I am. I wish he'd bloody well clear off home. It would make life a lot easier.

'He's just sailed through a film test in Rome, you know. I don't know why he doesn't take up acting, with his looks. He'd make more money, and I'd have nothing to worry about.'

After another look at his watch, about the tenth in as many minutes, he decided it was time to get ready, then changed his mind again when he registered that there was an hour and a half to go. He painstakingly polished his goggles instead, and all the time the music blared out from the radio. The yawns and expansive stretches were becoming more frequent. He glanced at his watch yet again and decided he might as well get ready after all. It would fill in the time.

He unzipped his black leather grip, the chalk-marks of scores of Customs men recalling his many trips abroad, and lifted out a ragged, well-worn suit of racing leathers. Then the wrinkled boots with the gaping holes on the instep and around the front of the soles. The famous white and gold helmet, chipped by flying stones, and kid gloves followed. There was no number on the back of the leathers—he couldn't be bothered to stitch it on. He slipped into a pair of navy blue ballet-tights and clowned a *pas-de-deux* on the bed before saying, 'I know I look a right twit in these, but they don't half keep you warm under the leathers.' A tee-shirt went on next. Across its front, in eye-catching black print, were the words *Pommie Bastards*. He explained, 'That keeps me well in when I go to South Africa. I had it made there.'

His chatter, in between yawns, was getting more animated. The tension was sharpening and he was beginning to enjoy the feeling, because he knew it would guarantee razor-like reactions and concentration.

He put the watch on the dressing-table, but in a place where he could see it easily. When he struggled into the skin-tight leathers, hitching his shoulders and twisting to get his body into them, it looked as if he was wrestling an invisible opponent.

He slumped on to the dressing-table stool, exhausted from the effort of yanking on the sleek leathers, and after yet another glance at his watch began once more the laborious polishing of goggles that were already crystal clear.

His need to fill in the waiting time by doing *anything* to ease the tension is almost a ritual. In between breathing on the glass and rubbing, he sighed, 'I'll be glad when it's all over. This is just about the worst part, waiting for the off. I think this is the time I'd willingly pack it all in. The only thing that stops me is that I know it'll soon be finished.'

Another glance at the expensive gold watch, another wipe of the goggles and a question he knew he really did not want to be answered. 'I should win here, don't you think? Trouble is, you never know with Ago. And that bike of mine's a mule to ride. It'd be better suited to show-jumping, it leaps about so much. I think I'll get Honda to enter it for the Grand National. It should stand a good chance. . . .'

In a flurry of wit, with a cruelly accurate take-off of a horse-race commentator, he chatters nasally through an imaginary microphone. 'And now Hailwood on Honda is safely over the last . . . he's running away with this race. . . . Honda has jumped magnificently. Nothing will catch them now. The Queen's horse just couldn't match Honda over these fences. . . .'

His levity, at this crucial stage of the build-up, was an illustration of his absolute preparedness.

He was now in complete control of himself, glowing with the sharpness of the great athlete, his tensions honed to a fine point. When he has steered himself through the early stages of his pre-race build-up, which are now so much a part of his daily life, and passed into this final phase, you feel you are looking at a tightly coiled spring. It is now, about about half an hour before the start of the race, that he retreats into his shell completely, and his concentration reaches its peak in his rigidly enforced disregard of the excitement around him. All his thoughts are aimed at the circuit, the competition, the opponents and the need for a fast, tactical getaway that will take him far into the lead.

One o'clock. Half an hour to go. The pavement beneath the hotel balcony is deserted. So are the beaches, despite the hot sun. Around the $37\frac{3}{4}$-mile macadam loop of the TT circuit almost 100,000 people are waiting, their thoughts centred on the afternoon's racing and on the two men in particular who are to provide what will certainly be its most memorable spectacle: Hailwood and Agostini.

Agostini has already passed the hotel, with a cheerful blast on the horn of his canary-coloured Porsche. Mike says, 'Ah well, here we go again.' Another visit to the lavatory, the hundredth yawn, and he picks up his helmet. Into it, as if it were a shopping-basket, go his gloves and his goggles. He grabs the radio, still playing, and strides out into the corridor.

Two paces, and he decides to turn back, with the smiling explanation, 'I'd better make sure my feet are clean enough to go to hospital.' Seconds later he is back again. 'They'll do. Too much washing is weakening. . . .'

A chambermaid, bending over a linen-basket outside a room, gets a smack on the bottom and turns round sharply on the offender. The glower fades when the culprit is revealed and she says, 'Oh, it's you . . . best of luck.'

All the way to the ground floor holiday-makers and hotel staff shout or whisper their good wishes, according to how close they are to Mike when he passes them. Every single one receives a 'thank you' in return, though Mike's concentration won't allow him to stop. He walks briskly out to his waiting car. The radio is still giving out pop music.

He roars away from the car park, arms at full stretch to the wheel in racing-driver fashion, and has the tyres bending from the wheel-rims as the borrowed BMW lurches from one corner to the next on the mile-long journey to the start. At the top of a steep hill just short of the circuit the road bends acutely to the right through an archway. Each time he goes through it he seems to try to put an extra mile an hour on as he slides through its narrow entrance.

Conversation on the drive to the circuit is, naturally, sparse and limited to observations about the weather. 'I could have done with some rain today instead of this sun. It would have kept the speed down a bit and brought the MV down to my level.'

There is another thought about the Honda. 'I don't think Honda pay me enough to ride this thing. It won't be the same next year. I'm going to screw them for all I can get out of them. It's hardly worth sticking my neck out like I do for the money I get.'

The circuit. Stretched out on the grass of Noble's Park are some spectators sunning themselves. Mike slides the car into an impossibly narrow-looking parking space. It has hardly glided to halt when it is surrounded by autograph-hunters, jostling, bustling and pestering at the time when they are least welcome. Only one, a grubby-looking little urchin, gets his programme signed. The rest are roughly brushed aside as Mike, head down, ears deaf, grim-faced, strides through the mêlée. His father, who has kept out of sight all morning, says briefly, 'Good luck . . . and be careful,' then makes his way to the grid.

The machines have been wheeled out of the lock-up tent where they have spent the night after being checked, and are being warmed up by the fussy mechanics. The sky-blue-suited Italians crowd round the MV. The grey overalls of the bristle-haired Japanese form a barrier around the big Honda.

The paddock is a cloud of blue smoke from a hundred exhausts. The noise is appalling, the shattering roar of a hundred multi- and single-cylinder engines warming up. The mechanics hover anxiously, relying more on their ears than on their eyes.

In the midst of the din Mike and Agostini chat unconcernedly in Italian, as tyre-fitters, chain-mechanics and other trade representatives dart to and fro through the crowd making final checks and offering good wishes. Race officials, with bits of paper in their hands, are busy trying to sort out who is placed where in the white-painted parenthesis marks on the grey concrete of the grid. The time-keepers, who will clock the time of every man, from first to last, are lined up behind a battery of stopwatches in a hut overlooking the start.

The silence, when it comes, is startling. With fifteen minutes to go the mechanics get the signal to stifle the deafening howl of the machines. Then comes the ceremonial wheeling-out, incongruously reminiscent of horses leaving the paddock at Royal Ascot.

The waiting queue of motor-cycles, each with its front wheel in one set of parenthesis marks, stretches away from the grandstand along the Glencrutchery road, on which, the day before, buses and cars were running.

Reports on weather- and road-conditions and potted biographies of the men lined up on the grid crackle through the Tannoy system. The white-helmeted policemen clear the area and the riders busy themselves by fussily tightening the straps on their boots, testing the brakes, tickling the carburettors—anything, in fact, to while away the remaining agonizing moments before they can really get down to work.

At the head of the queue, among the top riders seeded by ballot for leading positions so the slower men will not get in their way, Mike casually straddles the big Honda. Now he is completely sealed off in his shell. If people speak, he doesn't hear them. If they pat his back, he doesn't feel it.

He looks thoughtfully at Agostini's red MV, drawn up close by, and goes methodically over its lines, its engine, as if he were seeing it for the first time in his life—the machine that had carried him to world titles before the Italian took it over. Agostini, in his turn, is doing the same thing, looking across at the Honda. The world's two best riders on the fastest, most powerful machines in the business. A classic situation.

Behind them the rest of the riders will be racing in what is virtually a TT within the TT. They know that, barring accident or mechanical breakdown, the first two places will go to these two men. They are racing for the following places—a third place to them is as good as a first in their own TT.

The clockwork efficiency of the Japanese organization behind Mike has already moved smoothly into its stride. At the pits, in the shadow of a curious grandstand, chief mechanic Aika San, the most famous of all Japanese motor-cycle-racing experts, organizes his team. One man stands on a tool-box to get his head into the wooden-hooded telephone that is linked to others set up at critical stages of the course. Information is yelled to and fro over the phones so that Mike's progress is logged throughout the race. His time at every stage is relayed back to the pits, when Aika San expands it into a composite picture of the overall situation; he compares rival times, and passes the information on to Mike in chalked figures on a blackboard.

The amount of fuel to be piped into the tank, based on the distance in miles before the half-way mark fuel stop and the speed at which it will be covered, has already been computed. A mechanic with a spare pair of goggles slung around his neck practises and re-practises the speed at which he can refuel from the tank in the pits. Like a cowboy rehearsing a quick draw—not only quick, but accurate too. A fumble in the refuelling, a clumsy failure to get the nozzle into the tank first time, and valuable, hard-earned seconds can be thrown away.

The lid of the 500 cc mechanic's tool-box on the pits ledge is open already, before the race is underway, its contents gleaming, free from oil and grit. A newly washed pair of skin-tight gloves, without which the mechanic would never lay a finger on the machine, rest in the lid. A bottle of Coca-Cola stand ready in case Mike needs a drink at the third-lap halt. A sponge and a cleaning-cloth; new plugs in neat regiments.

The grid has been deserted by all but the riders. Trembling fingers tamper with the carbs, the brakes, the clutch. Pulses race, hearts beat quicker. Breathing is sharper.

The starter is climbing the two steps into the box. The minute-hand of the clock on the tall Dunlop tower jerks nearer to 1.30 p.m.

The flag is up—and fluttering down again in a blink. A maroon, heralding the start of the race, explodes in the expectant hush. Before its echo has faced, engines roar into ear-splitting life, the sound of the Honda's four cornet-shaped megaphones unmistakable among them.

Mike is at home now, moulding himself to the machine, the two already looking as if they had been tightly stitched together. He stretches out his legs to ease up the leathers so they don't grip around his knees and cause him discomfort. All his effort is concentrated on a searing first lap, piling on the pressure, demoralizing the opposition. It is a TT tactic that has paid off time after time—really, it is the only tactic.

Mike's father, with a chesnut tan from his winter and summer stays in Nassau and Cannes, steeples his fingers absent-mindedly into an attitude of prayer as he watches the marker-hands on the leader-board follow Mike's safe progress round the circuit. He feels more fear for his son than the son feels for himself, a fear that temporarily submerges the intense pride he has in Mike's skill. Relief comes only when he sees Mike pass under the chequered flag at the finish . . . whatever position he is in.

In the Press box, *Express* man Leslie Nichol turns to *Motor-Cycle News* editor Charlie Rous and says, 'This should be a bloody great race.' Professional excitement; no need to worry today how to fill the space they have been allotted.

Below them, just behind the tiny cage that forms Mike's pit, the feeling of involvement is more personal. Aika San, who rides every yard of the race without moving from his station, checks his stopwatch, scribbles out his calculation and grins widely. . . . He says laconically, 'Mike's going well.' In fact he has just broken the lap record from a standing start. From commentary points around the course the microphones pick up the sound of the Honda and pump it back to the grandstand. The mechanics stop their chatter and listen intently for any tell-tale off-key noises as the machine's whine reaches a crescendo, then trails off as Mike hurtles out of earshot.

The Shell helicopter waits in a field alongside the grid, primed to fly off at a moment's notice to airlift any accident cases from the course to the nearest hospital. Suddenly its rotors thresh into action, and Stan Hailwood, startled out of his meditations, says, 'Oh, Christ, where's that thing going? Where's Mike? Let's have a look.'

The marker on the leader-board gives the answer: he is safely through Ramsey, sped by a stream of superlatives from the commentator. 'Thank the Lord,' Stan sighs, adding, 'I hope Mike doesn't do anything stupid. I don't know why the hell I come here year after year just to get the life scared out of me. I wonder if Mike will pack it all in this year. I can't stand much more of this.'

He doesn't know it, but Mike's in trouble. His times give no indication. The hitch is revealed when he shoots true and straight as an arrow into the pits at the end of the third lap. The filler cap is already propped up. In one sweep his hand rips off the fly-spattered goggles and puts on the fresh, clear pair.

The petrol-pipe nozzle plunges into the tank as the mechanic's eye scrutinizes the now silent Honda. Mike remains astride it. Casually, almost nonchalantly, he points at the handlebars and says, 'The bloody twist-grip keeps falling off. It's frightening the knickers off me.'

Stan Hailwood, almost anonymous in the crowd pressing against the railings behind the pits, yells, 'What's the matter? What's wrong?'

Above: The winner, Mike, a privateer, with Honda works men Tom Phillis (*far left*) and Taveri, at the 1961 250 cc TT.

In the winner's enclosure, 1961. Now you can see who Mike gets his nose from!

52

Top left: Mike's first try-out on a works MV, September 1961. In the background: Bill Webster, the man who helped Mike in the early days; Nello Pagani, the MV competitions manager, and Dickie Brown.

Below left: Tough going in the Scottish Six Days Trial.

Above right: The Ecurie Sportive workshop at Mike's Oxford home.

Below right: Polishing some of the pots.

Balance . . .

. . . is the thing.

Mike demonstrating the art of throwing a bike about—however big it is.

MV mechanic Vittorio Carrano—he wept when Mike left to join Hondas.

Ruefully Mike explains, grabbing a mallet from a mechanic and starting to hammer the twist-grip back on. The treatment is in vain. The grip needs taking down and tacking on properly, but there is no time. The vital seconds are ebbing away. A mechanic knots a handkerchief over the troublesome stretch of rubber in a makeshift bid to anchor it in place. Aika San shakes his head. Mike merely shrugs resignedly, accepting his bad luck.

Stan Hailwood shouts, 'Come on, get off the thing! Quit now. It's madness to go on.' He receives a steely stare and Mike's answer, 'You must be joking.' The filler-lid snaps back into place, Mike's powerful shoulders heave the Honda forward, it fires sweetly and he is gone.

Onlookers rush away to tell their friends about the trouble. Information about the problem Mike is faced with crackles over the Tannoy and 100,000 people share his worries.

Stan Hailwood turns away and comes face to face with Aika San. 'He must be mad . . . he must be mad.' Aika San smiles wanly.

The delay has cost Mike eleven seconds—seconds surrendered to Agostini, who is performing superbly. 'He'll never do it,' Stan mutters, knowing nevertheless that if his son does do it the glory will be greater. But at the same time not wanting him to try. A lesser man than Mike would have pulled out, with as much justification as he needed to gloss over failure. There would have been no criticism. But for Mike the setback only strengthens his will to win whatever the odds.

Bill Ivy, Mike's friend and the 125 cc world champion, bites his nails and tries to put himself in Mike's place. 'That grip could slide off on any corner and Mike'll find himself with a handful of thin air. It'll have him off unless he's careful. He'll have to watch it all the way.'

Mike, meanwhile, is sticking his neck out so far that he has no time to be frightened. Over the limit, quicker than any other man has ridden round the island's tortuous course. The forgiving nature of the circuit has never been so sorely tried; and the eleven-second gap is closing. Mike tops Agostini's effort by one second—then loses it again. He falls back, the twist-grip popping off the end of the handlebars at virtually every turn in the road. But he keeps going.

It looks as if Mike is to be robbed of his twelfth TT and the Italian is going to score his first 500 cc win.

Agostini swoops round Windy Corner, the finish only a few miles distant. Then without any warning the MV, which up to now has never faltered in its stride, suddenly slithers to a full stop. Agostini climbs off and looks down at the road; the chain, scorched free of grease, has broken up. The links, like red-hot fragments of shrapnel, are scattered across the macadam. The Italian is powerless to do anything about it: Mike has only to keep going to win.

Back at the pits Vic Doyle, the Reynolds Chain representative, wipes his brow. He can't hide his feelings. 'It wasn't one of ours!' Joyfully he tells everybody he meets, 'It wasn't ours. Oh dear me, what a relief! I'd have never lived it down.' Dunlop man Derek Carpenter knows the feeling. One of his tyres once inexplicably punctured pancake flat and robbed Mike of a win in the Spanish. . . .

Mike can't believe his luck. He is desperately tired, with the washed-out look of a man who by his own effort has just thrown off all the worries and tensions in the world. Back in the pits, now, he is still shaking, blinking, wrinkling his face to iron out the deep trenches the framework of the goggles has made under his eyes. His nose is bloody from flying stones, the soles of his boots have been scraped clear of leather so that his toes show through—clear evidence of the Honda's terrifying angle of lean. The mechanics can't hide their delight; they pump his hand and vigorously slap his back, giving the lie to their reputation for being inscrutable and unemotional.

Mike's father offers his congratulations, and adds, 'I'll see you at the car.' Walking through the staring crowd, he tells me, 'We were lucky today, very lucky. It's hard luck for Ago, but we've had enough bad luck this year and it had to move out sooner or later. Look at me—my hands are still shaking.'

Bill Ivy joins us at the car. 'What a character, that Oilwood! He's gone for a ride in the helicopter now.' Above us the helicopter spins round, Mike waves, then is transported out of sight for a bird's-eye view of the course. Half an hour later he's back. 'Home, James—and take it easy. Don't go rushing about all over the place.' No mention of the trouble he has had, that comes later.

Mike sang in the bath, squirted water up the tiles, nibbled chicken sandwiches in wet fingers and adeptly turned the taps on and off with his toes. 'Are we going to have a night tonight, half a night or a night and a half? One thing's sure: I am going to get stoned, well and truly tottery.'

Then, seriously, 'Jeez, did I stick my neck out today! Still, look at the money. It's better than working.' The leathers, the goggles, helmet and gloves were scattered in aimless confusion around the bedroom floor. The goggles which only a few hours earlier had been treated with such loving care.

Instead of the working gear, the immaculate clothing for a night out now absorbed his careful attention. His face shone, his thin damp hair was carefully combed to hide as much skin as possible. A midnight blue double-breasted suit from Savile Row, a hand-made shirt, a flowery tie and boots high over the ankle. The man about town, looking far removed from the popular conception of racing motor-cyclists as a legion of unwashed tearaways.

The vodkas-and-lemonades followed one another down the Hailwood throat; not small measures, doubles. The barman, looking on when he could spare the time from serving the most continuous flow of customers, observed, 'You deserve it.'

There was a dinner in honour of Mike and Agostini, thrown by the hotel. They sat at the head of the table, laughing and joking as if the afternoon had never happened; a picture of friendliness. Mike gleefully taught Agostini an obscene phrase connected with old boots, and was left with watering eyes and aching sides when the Italian, not knowing what he was saying, repeated it loudly enough for the majority of the guests to hear.

Half-way through the dinner Mike broke off to go to the Palace dance-hall, where the *Daily Mirror* Man-of-the-Week award was to be made. By now the volume of vodka was taking effect. He sprinted across the car park, clicking his heels in the air as he went.

When he was presented on stage in front of three thousand people he burst through the net curtain from the wings like something out of a horror film, crouching, arms flung wide, knees bent. The crowd loved the clowning, and cheered his honesty when, in response to the announcer's question, 'What are you going to do now?' he boomed into the microphone, 'I am going to get stoned.' Commissionaires and Palace security men had to clear a path through the crowd when he made his way towards the hotel. He was forced to a dead stop, signing autographs on girls' arms, programmes, diaries and letters. They whooped after him all the way in the hundred-yard dash back to the safety of the hotel. He threw the trophy—a silver salver— over to me and said, 'Here, you can have it. You've done more work than me this week. It'll do for you to put your collar-studs on.'

When we returned, Agostini was still trying to discover the full extent of his *faux pas*. The air was blue with Neapolitan oaths when Mike explained. Soon they were in the Casino together, Mike gambling fifty pounds a time on the blackjack table . . . and winning. The last time I saw him that night, he was deeply engrossed with a long-haired blonde girl who was gazing at him with adoring eyes. But it wasn't the last time I heard him. . . .

I woke up at about four in the morning to the sound of laughter and splashes coming from the hotel swimming-pool below my bedroom window. I could hear the *Daily Sketch* man, Jimmy Nicholson, shouting, 'No, Mike! No! I've got my best suit on.' Then a splash. Then all was quiet until I heard a knock at my door and a familar voice whispering, 'Ted, get up. Come and have a drink.'

'I don't want that sort of drink. Clear off,' I said. He did, but a few minutes later a group of Casino security men were surrounding the pool, shouting, 'Now come on, Mr Hailwood, be reasonable. Come on out.' 'Come on in and get us,' came the good-humoured answer, 'the water's lovely.' Two newspapermen, still fully dressed in sopping wet lightweight suits, staggered out and slopped their way to their bedrooms muttering, 'Mad . . . mad . . . the man's mad.' The men in the pool were stripped down to their underpants, the girls to bras and panties. One of the girls worked in the Casino and was sacked for her part in Mike's wild bid to let his hair down; but he interceded on her behalf and managed to get her reinstated.

Saturday morning. The TT had come and gone. Crowds streamed towards the boats and planes in a non-stop procession from breakfast-time. Buses were running again on their usual routes, which for the past week had echoed to the roar of thoroughbred racing machinery. Riders, their vans loaded with bikes and accessories, were setting off for the next world-championship round at Assen in Holland.

Back at the hotel, Mike slept late. He awoke to the normal anticlimax of TT week; the feeling of emptiness after a spell without a minute to spare, without a speck of privacy.

There was a restless look about him, an inability to sit or stand in one place for too long. All the immediate targets and ambitions had been removed; the next peak to scale was a week away, the Dutch TT. He had to find something to relieve the boredom that had replaced the tension. . . .

'A game of golf, that's it,' he said brightly. A few phone calls, and a fourball was laid on at the Pulrose course, near the Quarter Bridge section of the TT circuit.

There was a hair-raising drive to the course, a violent four-wheel slide into the club's forecourt and we were there. Mike, a good golfer who could be brilliant if he gave it more time, slammed the ball and vented his feelings for half the course, then was suddenly bored by it all. With mischievous inventiveness, which would have had him thrown out on his ear had it been seen by a course official, he devised a race with the golf trolleys.

They scampered down the steeper hills, feet on the axles, pushing with alternate feet to get up speed, the handles facing forwards and clubs spilling out all over the place. The Saturday-morning golfers looked on in horror as the four madmen pushed and weaved and bored each other with complete lack of care for each other's safety. The fact that a leg, an arm or a skull could have been fractured was disregarded in the orgy of relaxed tension. The romp ended when the four men were breathless, less from the effort of pushing than from laughter.

One had the feeling, watching the hilarious performance, that there was an attitude among these men that had been present, years ago, in the Battle-of-Britain pilots. Devil-may-care men to whom nothing in the way of relaxation and relief is too outrageous; childlike and refreshing, offending nobody and nothing but convention. I have seen Mike hanging upside down by his legs from a branch of a tree in an endurance contest against other riders; there have been marathon conker tournaments that have threatened to crack knuckles with their energetic swipes.

They could all be dismissed as mentally unbalanced, but when you consider the severity of the tension under which they live their wildness becomes easier to understand, and tolerance, too, is easier. They live dangerously, and relax dangerously too. Mike, for instance, finds it extremely difficult to drive round London without subconsciously trying to set up a new lap record for Hyde Park Corner. During his annual holiday in South Africa he races GT cars and gives what amount almost to demonstration rides on an ageing Honda. His search for new outlets for his energies in between races is seemingly endless; the vacuum that separates one season from another is welcome at the beginning, but it soon loses its attraction and the wait becomes intolerable.

Four miles along the ocean highway out of Nassau city is a pink-painted house that nestles in the lee of its own jetty and faces south-east towards Cat Island, overlooking the warm sea that washes the beaches of the Bahamas. This is the haven Mike escapes to after the exhausting rigours of a season's racing; the place where he slows himself down.

The house, with its spacious lounge and the deep window that gives a panoramic view of the speedboats and yachts as they skim round tiny Cat Island, is normally Mike's last call in the lull between one season and the next.

He explained, 'If I stopped racing tomorrow I would have enough to live on for the rest of my life. I'm not really wealthy, but I suppose I'm comfortably off. And the money I have has been earned by my own labours. Nobody has given me anything; I've had to work for it like anyone else, and work bloody hard.

'By the time the season's finished, what with all the racing and travelling, I've had enough; I feel knocked out, and even more so during my time with Honda. I get an urge to clear off, as far away as I can from the atmosphere of the racing world. That, in a nutshell, is why I bought the house.

'I spend quite a lot of time in the Bahamas, so I decided I might as well have a place of my own. This spot is ideal and a great rest cure. I bought it as soon as I saw it—it really is in a beautiful setting. And what's the point of throwing money away by staying in hotels? Stan uses the place when I'm not there.

'I normally stop over in Nassau after I've been to America, or on my way back from Japan if I've been testing. The rest works wonders, tones me up for the oncoming season.

'When the Grand Prix season winds up, I start the first leg of my relaxation course. Usually I take a bike to South Africa and mix it in with some GT racing, a paid holiday in the sunshine. Then I like to pop across to Finland or to Luigi Taveri's chalet in Switzerland to get in some skiing; nothing keeps you fitter than that. Nassau comes next, whenever I can fit it in.

'I must say, though, that by the time the season is due to start I've usually had enough of the loafer's life. I get bored very quickly; idling around on a sunny beach is all right up to a point, but with nothing more to do than get a tan the time doesn't half drag.

'It sounds ideal, doesn't it? All that sunshine and swimming. I suppose there are millions of people to whom this would be the perfect existence, but not me. The job I am in makes me too restless to feel the same way about it as other people. I would hate to vegetate.

'This is what worries me about quitting motor-cycle racing; it's such a full life. When I do turn it in there will never be enough for me to do to fill in the time. This, as much as anything, is why I've gone into the house-building business in South Africa along with Frank Perris. At least it'll give me something to think about.

'I get to the stage where I can't sit still for a minute. If I'm here I want to be there. When I'm there I want to be somewhere else, and the thought of spending any time with people who aren't interested in the same things as me drives me potty. I'm terribly inflexible that way; I can't even feign interest if I'm bored.

'I don't think I'm peculiar in this respect; I think most of the boys in the motor-cycle-racing business feel the same way. This is probably why we're a clannish lot; people outside the circle can't appreciate what we feel, can't understand what we're talking about and generally don't know the difference between a Grand Prix and a Grand National. The need to keep moving doesn't affect other people quite as much as us. It's annoying, for instance, to have to halt in the middle of a conversation to explain to somebody who really isn't interested just who Ubbiali was.

'Let's face it, we speak a different language. Even half the organizers and most of the officials at the FIM don't understand us. We sit in a tight circle and anybody outside it really is well and truly outside. It's pretty much the same in the car world; even though I raced cars I was hardly ever a member of the inner circle.'

It is enlightening to sit, say, in the Castrol caravan in the paddock at a Continental circuit after a race. Riders, and any trade representatives who can spare the time, pile in to sit and drink and discuss, with almost childlike enthusiasm, the yard-by-yard happenings on the circuit. The riders sit bare-chested, with their leathers rolled down to their waists, showing the scars and stitch-marks of previous spills. Their palms raw and skinned from hanging tightly onto bouncing bikes, their toes are visible through gashes in their boots, ripped open on hundreds of corners. Untidy hair is plastered down under sweaty helmets, noses and cheeks are bloody from flying stones. Everybody in turn analyses his own race, catalogues his own near misses.

In Italy, after practice at Monza, Rex Butcher burst in on one of these typical get-togethers. He was visibly agitated, his face dark and serious. He stared at Mike and said, 'You've just frightened the life out of me.' He wiped his brow and went on emphatically, 'Oh, mate, don't ever do that again!'

'Do what again?' Mike thought he must have cut across Rex's path—but he couldn't remember doing it.

'Scare me like that. I was following you through the top end of the circuit. That bloody camel you ride'—he pointed vaguely towards where the big Honda was garaged—'swung right out. It almost jack-knifed. The back end came right over; I thought you were off. And you must have been bobbing on a bit through there. I'll tell you this much, I wouldn't ride that thing for a ransom. You can have it for me. Is the suspension wrong or something?'

Mike said with a grin, 'For a minute I thought you were going to tell me something serious. I thought I'd chopped you on the bend. Yes, it does that all the time. All *you* have to do is keep clear, you can leave the rest to me. I'm sorry if it gave you a turn; try imagining what it does to me.' Rex walked away shaking his head.

Mike, the incident forgotten in an instant—it happened too often to be particularly memorable—went back to telling us how he had brought an abrupt end to a prize presentation party by stuffing a potted plant into the end of a trombone.

When he is overcome by the urge to be mischievous Mike can be outrageous. The more outrageous, the more the riders enjoy it.

'I remember coming up behind Mike Duff in a TT. He was in a world of his own, wrapped up in his own problems, head down behind the screen, backside sticking up in the air. He didn't hear me coming, he thought he was all alone. I pulled up alongside him and clouted his bottom. You should have seen the look on his face, he almost shot out of his leathers.

'Then, at Aintree, I worked a terrible trick on Derek Minter. I was only about seventeen, so my cunning must have developed early.

'I had a quicker bike than Derek's, but he was outriding me in a great big dice. We were on the last lap and heading towards the final turn; I knew I'd never beat him by fair means. I managed to draw up alongside him, and when he looked across I pointed frantically to his back wheel as if there was something wrong with it. There wasn't, of course, but he shut off and screwed his head backwards to have a look. By the time he'd turned round again I'd gone. I won, and he wasn't too happy about it.

'I'm not proud of that. I regretted it afterwards and I've never done anything like it since.'

When the laughter subsided, Bill Ivy said, 'No, you don't have to now.'

In my account of Mike's schooldays I mentioned his lifelong interest in music. It is curiously uncharacteristic of him that he suppresses his talent in this direction, refusing to play any of the instruments he has mastered for anybody but himself or a few close friends.

This is one of the rare respects in which the introverted side of his character has the upper hand. His showmanship and confidence—the other side of him—come to the fore in his racing and in the clothes he wears, which are a compromise between Carnaby Street at its most garish and Savile Row at its most conservative.

In his appreciation of music, again, he is the complete extrovert. He dances with unwitting exhibitionism, jacket off, shirt-sleeves rolled up, tie unknotted and hanging loose, wherever he is, at a house party or in a nightclub.

He enthuses about music and sits for hours talking about rhythm to his firm friend Chris Barber, the jazz-band leader. When he is in New York he will never leave without having visited Birdland. In Paris he spends hours in the jazz and beat cellars.

His London flat is almost as well equipped as a BBC radio studio; there are hi-fis, stereos, tape-recorders and miles of tapes, towering columns of records. There is a radio in the bedroom, another in the bathroom and one in the lounge.

His car is like an extension of the flat, with a tape-recorder, fixed in alongside the radio, and a small library of cassettes.

'I don't know how people could ever live without music,' said Mike. 'Wherever I am, the room has to be filled with music. As soon as I get up in the morning the radio goes on. I wouldn't dream of going for a night out to a place where there was no music, even if it was only a piano tinkling in the corner.'

Mention of a piano took me back to a night in a hotel at Assen where the Dutch TT had been staged. The racing had finished, and Mike and I toured the town trying to find a bar or a club where there would be music to listen to. All we could find were bands that featured accordions or bird-warblers, hardly easy on a jazz-lover's ear. Mike was looking for something more relaxing.

Two hours—and a few vodkas—later, he decided he had had enough of searching and headed back towards his hotel in the town centre. There he was delighted to find the manager picking out tunes on the smooth-sounding piano in the cocktail-lounge. It was then shortly after midnight.

A few more riders and friends drifted in, until there were a dozen of us sitting drinking and listening to the pianist, who could imitate George Shearing or Oscar Petersen to a degree where you could hardly tell the difference. Mike was completely enchanted by the man's talent and feel for music. He sat stock-still, eyes riveted on the fingers that glided over the keyboard. He spoke only to suggest a tune now and again.

At 5 a.m., with the dawn beginning to show through the window, the pianist started on a George Shearing number. Mike leaned across his table and whispered, much louder than he had intended, 'I'd give twenty thousand pounds to be able to play like that.'

The man swivelled round on the piano stool and looked incredulously towards the voice. Along with something like 200,000 other people he had that afternoon watched Mike win a race in stirring fashion, shattering the lap record en route. He had seen the adulation and heard the cheers. And here was that idol—the man *he* would willingly have swapped places with—saying that he wished he had the pianist's talent.

He didn't know that Mike could play, until after much badgering the champion sat at the keyboard, his defences no doubt softened by the vodkas. Mike sat and played, and the pianist said, 'I reckon you don't need to spend twenty thousand pounds.' Mike was both flattered and embarrassed. That was the last time I heard Mike play the piano 'in public', if a small, intimate party qualifies for that description.

Part of Mike's luggage used to be a clarinet, a portable gramophone and a pile of Sydney Bechet records. He used to relax before a race by sitting on the bed, in his leathers, playing the clarinet accompaniment to his Bechet discs. At times he was so wrapped up in the music that his mechanics, or his father, had to hammer on the door to remind him he was in danger of being late for the race.

'I don't take it with me now,' he said, 'too many people in the hotel used to complain about the din. It must have sounded dreadful; people must have wondered who the lunatic was blowing his lungs out on a clarinet each morning. They should think themselves lucky I didn't play the sousaphone or the trombone.

'You know, outsiders think I lead a wild life, *dolce vita* and all that. They'd be shocked to have seen me sitting at home in the flat, puffing away on the clarinet, tape-recording it and playing it back. Then blowing again until I'd got it right, which was very rarely. If Bechet only knew what I used to do to his music!

'It must be a good life being a musician; doing something you really enjoy, getting around, never still, and all those birds. The only trouble is the money's not so good; half of them are scratching round for a living. I wouldn't fancy that part of it. Still, I think that if I wasn't what I am, that's what I'd like to be.'

7 Honda

Mike brought a new dimension to motor-cycle racing when he left Count Agusta to join Soichiro Honda's highly successful works team. In a word, the dimension was 'Hondamanship'. An art within an, art a new skill within the complexities of multi-cylinder motor-cycle racing. It was the knack of taming the built-in Honda waywardness, especially in the 500 cc machine, and still achieving success. He had to ride faster, harder, than ever before on machinery whose handling was not designed to withstand the tremendous power of the engines. The frame simply could not cope.

His experience, especially with the big, ungainly but awesomely powerful 500, left Mike with the impression that he was living even more dangerously than usual. His feeling was that week after week he was risking his life to an extent that frightened him far more than any other episode of his career had done.

In the long time I have known him, I have never seen him as nervy as he was after joining Honda. It is remarkable that, despite his apprehensions, he achieved a series of breathtaking results. With sheer riding skill and courage he had to compensate for the shortcomings of the machinery. He had to battle constantly against brilliant opposition and, at the same time, fight against what should have been his one ally— the machine underneath him. The manner in which he got the results was often more impressive than the results themselves. It is important to realize the extent of what he achieved after he moved over to Hondas.

With characteristic candour Mike described his feelings about the Hondas he had to ride. He said, 'I really enjoyed racing the 250, even though the Yamahas I raced against were quicker. The 250 was quite well behaved and easy to handle. The 350 was okay, too. When I rode it I was within my capabilities. But every time I rode the 500 I used to think, on the morning before the race, I wish I didn't have to ride in this event. I wish it wasn't on.

'It wasn't just the usual matter of trying to win, it was trying to stay on the thing. It really was the most frightening experience. I could stick my neck out on the 250; I could really have a go and not be worried for a second. I could dice all the way with Bill Ivy and Phil Read on their Yamahas, and even though the Honda was streets slower I enjoyed the racing. But to try anything at all on the 500 I felt I was risking my life. I had no confidence in the bike. I had to concentrate all the time on keeping it stable. I had trouble with it at almost every point of a circuit: into corners and out of them, on the straights, winding it on over the bumpy bits. It whipped like mad and bent in the middle. Then it wobbled all over the road.

'It only had a half-loop frame, a sort of moped frame, onto which the engine was bolted. The motor and loop formed the mainstay of rigidity. But there was really nothing rigid about it. Honda welded struts onto it almost every week to strengthen it, but it didn't make any difference.

'The front brake was big and heavy, and that didn't help when the bike started to get up to its tricks; the weight used to accentuate the lack of control. Whenever I put the power on over bumps I could feel the bike twisting underneath me. It felt as if the front end was at right-angles to the back. It was impossible to control it or steer it the way I wanted to go. Other riders often told me after a race or practice that they didn't know how I stayed on it. They said, "You should have seen it at such-and-such a place. Rather you than me!"

'The design was basically wrong. The instability came from the tremendous power of the engine setting up reactions through the frame.

'I can't understand why Honda, with all their money and technical know-how, failed to rectify that fault. It seems they had a blind spot on the question of frames. They reasoned that if they made the fastest motor in the business there was no reason why the rider shouldn't win. If the Honda got beaten they simply developed another engine with more power.

'They must have spent a fortune on new engines—and in all fairness they were terrific—but they failed to realize that for a fraction of the cost they could have developed a decent frame.'

Mike's struggle to find a cure went on behind the scenes as well. He spent hours alone—and hours more with Colin Lyster, a former racer and frame expert—trying to find the answer. He sent a Norton frame to Japan for the factory to examine. The research and development men tried a Honda engine in it, but of course it was a failure. The Norton frame, perfect for its own engine, which produced about fifty horse-power, was completely unsuitable with the power of the higher-rated Honda flooding through it.

'I spent ages trying to figure out an answer,' said Mike. 'Colin Lyster, who had worked on the Paton frames, which seemed to handle okay, offered his help.

'When I spoke to a chap from Renolds, the tube-makers, he said it would take a couple of months to knock up a new frame. That was far too long to have to wait, so Colin and I went to Italy to see a man who had a welding business just outside Milan. Everybody told us he was a brilliant welder and a fair hand with frames. I took the best tubing I could find and a Honda engine. He really got to work and produced a frame in sixteen days. We almost lived on his doorstep to make sure he hurried things along.

'We put the engine in it and tested it at Modena. It wasn't too bad, but it still wasn't quite right. Though we knew we were on the right lines. It was certainly steadier, and I could throw the bike around far more than I could with the Honda frame. But it obviously needed more time: we needed to get the suspension settings right and the fork angles sorted out.

'I rode the Honda with new, fuller frame at Rimini before the Grand Prix season started. I managed to win, and the frame stood up to the tougher test better than the standard one would have done. It was obviously only a question of time before the new frame was absolutely right, but time was something I didn't have enough of. I couldn't risk using it in the world championships.

'The fact that I was trying out a new frame leaked out to the motorcycle Press, and Honda were furious. They sent me a strong letter emphasizing that they like to keep everything they do secret. But I still couldn't get them to commit themselves about making a better frame. Then it all came to a head when I asked them for some bits and pieces for the new unit. They were so slow in responding that I gave up and abandoned the idea.

'They knew as well as I did that I couldn't afford to use it in the championships, so it stayed in my van. It cost me more than a thousand pounds, and I'm still convinced that it could have been successful if Honda had given me some assistance; I couldn't do it alone.

'The old Hondas, the ones in use in 1961, were bad handlers compared with other bikes. In the light of their history of atrocious handling, Jim Redman comes out as a far better rider than most people are prepared to give him credit for. To my mind he's twice as good as anybody ever rated him; he deserved every one of his titles. Nobody would have had to work harder for them than he did. Jim had been riding Hondas for years and never said anything about the handling. I suppose he accepted it at first then, in the end, believed it was natural. He probably thought it was a power wobble rather than a fault. If he'd really put his foot down and insisted that something was done, then the big Honda wouldn't have become such a nightmare.

'Let's face it, money should buy perfection in machinery. With Honda's will to succeed I'm surprised they didn't realize they were beating themselves by standing still on the issue of frames.

'Despite all the problems I'd signed a contract and I just had to do the best I could. When it came to signing again in 1967 I stipulated that the frames should be put right. Honda promised me they'd see to it, and so I signed the contract; but the new frames never materialized.'

It is Mike's view that he risked his neck on the big Honda every time he rode it; I have seen him reduced to near collapse, shaking and jumpy after races all over Europe. We all feel afraid for him.

Once I saw a young woman, sick with fright, ask her husband to drive her back to their hotel after she had just seen Mike skilfully tame a particularly fearsome wobble. Then, in the Isle of Man, at the bottom of the notorious Bray Hill, four men agreed to go and watch at another less terrifying section of the course.

I was standing near them when we heard the familiar howl of the Honda as Mike headed towards Bray, just after Pit Straight. Mike was piling it on down Bray, a steep, bumpy ski-run of a hill, at around 130 m.p.h., when the bike began to wobble. He shot up from the saddle, stood upright on the footrests and wrestled with the handlebars, like a rough-rider trying to bring down a steer by its horns. It was a heart-stopping moment and it was all over in a flash, but it left the crowd cold with fear.

'It must have seemed a spectacular method of dealing with the problem but it was the only way out of it,' said Mike. 'Moments like that happened so often that I began to get used to them. I got to the stage where I thought there was something wrong with the bike if it ever failed to misbehave.'

Mike, sitting in his flat near London Airport, said, 'When I first wanted to join Honda a few years ago they didn't want me. It made me feel slighted; I felt they were insulting me by turning me down. Then when I eventually did join the team I wasn't so sure I'd done the right thing.

'Things were going badly for me towards the end of the '64 season; I was very dissatisfied with life and undecided about my future. I was getting fed up with MVs—I was always being blown off by Jim Redman's 350 Honda and Count Agusta wouldn't build another bike.

'I pestered him but he was adamant. I was really having to struggle against Jim, but it didn't make any difference to the Count's way of thinking. My 500 was going perfectly and that was all that seemed to matter to him. I longed for more competitive racing than I was getting on the 500. There was nothing really to race against, and I was becoming terribly bored.

'After a while the Count must have realized I was getting to the end of my tether, because he told me he was making another 350, but nothing came of it. By the end of the year my disappointment was at a peak. Then, out of the blue, Jim asked me if I'd like to swap over to Honda. I assumed he'd been briefed to make the approach, and that Honda were really interested in having me on their side. I told Jim that if he could fix it I would sign—and I didn't care about the money. It was a case of swings and roundabouts. I knew I could lose money on the basic contract, but also that I would get more rides and make up the cash that way.

'Jim tried to get me a ride in the 1964 Italian Grand Prix at Monza and I really built up my hopes. But Honda said 'no' without giving any reasons. It shocked me and upset me more than I showed at the time. The factory I most wanted to ride for simply didn't want to know me. I thought it was the end of any chance I might have to ride the Hondas. I thought that perhaps they were holding a grudge against me from 1961. At that time, when Tom Phillis and Jim Redman were in the team and trying to keep everybody else out, I'd been given a Honda 250 on a loan basis. I blew the team men off and won the world championship. I think they would have given me another Honda for the following season, but at the time I wanted to ride for MV more than anything else. Consequently we didn't ask Honda for another bike. Apparently this upset them; and they operate an unwritten rule that once you leave them there is no going back.

'But what a difference in three years! In '64 I was moaning because

'he Honda mechanics working
ırough an all-night session at
Ionza. Chief mechanic Aika San,
ɔending) is on the right.

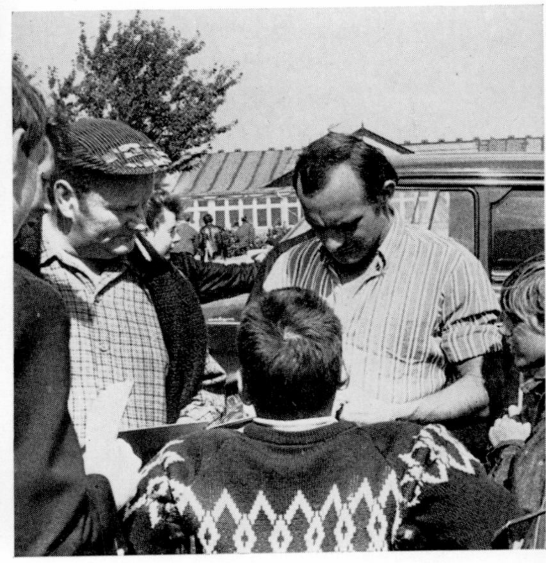

Above right and below:
Two moods . . . Autographing at
Brands Hatch.

The eyes of a man of speed;
detatchment, concentration, poise.

At Brands for his first car race. Mike sitting in his Formula Junior Brabham.

In South Africa with Graham Hill and motor-cycle ace Paddy Driver.

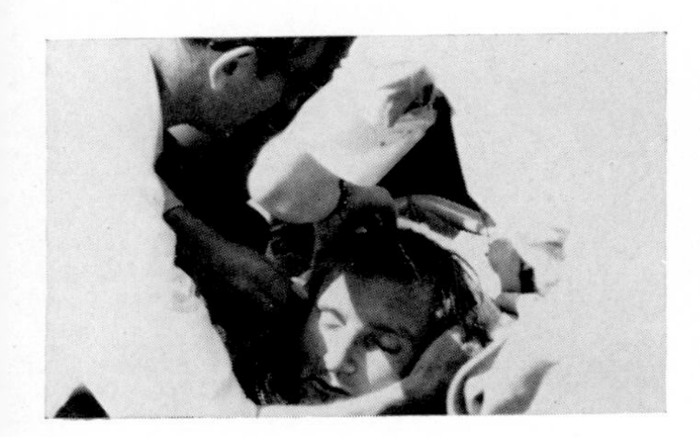

After this spill in East Germany Mike woke up in hospital and quipped: 'It's a good job I only fell on my head—otherwise I might have hurt myself.'

At the Nürburgring, 1964. Motor racing was starting to become a bore to Mike.

Top: Planning the book with Ted Macauley at Hockenheim.

Below left and right: 'Racing has made me an old man before my time.' . . . Five years' difference from the 1962 TT to the 1967 Ulster Grand Prix.

I wasn't getting enough rides. By '67 I was getting too many. I should have stayed with MV.

'The main thing about Honda was that you could always rely on them to dig out something special when it was needed. It made the prospect of riding for them extremely attractive. To my mind they were the tops in the business, way ahead of the field. There wasn't a rider in the world who'd have turned down a chance to race for them.

'I suppose that when I first wanted to join them my enthusiasm came at an inopportune time. I would have been a luxury they could well have done without; they were doing quite nicely without needing to strengthen their line-up. Jim was winning everything in sight on the 250 and 350, and the 500 was still a few sketchy lines on the drawing-boards.

'But if Honda didn't want me, MV did—and so did another Japanese factory, Suzuki. At the Japanese Grand Prix, where I rode an East German 250 MZ, Suzuki, through Frank Perris, asked me if I'd like to join them. I went to the factory for talks and a look round, but I didn't fancy riding two-strokes. The bike was very quick but it wasn't reliable enough for my liking. It also had the unnerving habit of seizing, so much so that the Aussie rider Jack Ahearn named it 'Whispering Death'. I turned down the offer and hoped that Count Agusta would spend some time developing a 350 so I could have a real go at Jim's Honda.

'At the start of 1965 I flew to Italy to see the Count and sign for another year. I didn't really want to, but I reasoned that with the 500 MV it was at least easy money. I was still smarting from being turned down by Honda, and this, as much as anything, influenced my decision to stay with MV.

'The 250 racing looked like a good thing to be in and I fancied it very much. Jim and Phil Read were having some titanic battles and I felt left out of it. The only time I managed to get in was when I went to the East German and raced a 250 MZ.

'My races on the 500 were, by comparison, walk-overs. I was often left with only the clock to race against; there was nothing else around to match the MV.

'The Count had an old 250 hidden away in the factory; it had been built in 1959, and when Provini, Ubbiali and Gary Hocking had raced it they had left everything else limping along behind them. I persuaded the Count to let me try it, but when we aired it, it was beaten out of sight.

Basically it was a superb bike, but obviously out of date. I asked Count Agusta to develop it, and he said the factory intended to make one in the future but he had his hands full trying to infuse more life into the 350.

'As the year went on Honda hit a bad patch. They tried Alan Shepherd, but he got hurt and very nearly killed in a spill in Japan. And I still had no idea I was in the running to join the team. When Alan was invited over it seemed to me I had been completely by-passed.

'One morning towards the end of '65, shortly before the Japanese Grand Prix, when the usual heap of mail dropped through my letter-box, tucked away in the middle of it all was a letter with a Japanese stamp on it. It was from Honda. I looked at it for ages without thinking about opening it; I tried to find a dozen reasons why they should be writing to me, without even considering the obvious one.'

'When I did open it, it said, "DEAR SIR, I congratulate you bring about good results. Now, as in my opinion, I hope reply whether you are will ride in Honda 6 (250 cc) at '65 Japan GP race or not. I recommend in an instant for Honda Motor, Co., Ltd. I await reply."

'It was signed by H. Sekiguchi, the director of Research and Development at Honda. His grammar may have been shaky, but the message was plain. I gathered that they only wanted to try me out, but I thought it could be the first step towards signing a contract with them. They swore me to secrecy, and even though I was bursting to tell somebody I had to keep quiet about the offer.

'The one man I did tell was Count Agusta. He still held my contract, which wasn't due to expire until January 1966. At first he said I could race the Honda, then he changed his mind and refused permission. Just when I was really despairing, he changed his mind once more and said it would be okay. I was delighted. I knew that it was a good chance and that it was up to me to make sure I didn't flunk it. But I tried not to build up my hopes; I didn't want to be disappointed again.

'When I rode the 250 for the first time I couldn't believe how badly it handled. I thought it was just about the worst thing I'd ever ridden, and I put my views over rather strongly. I told them it was bloody awful.

'It was an eye-opener for me; I couldn't understand how Jim had got through the season, racing hard against Phil Read, on such a thing.

'After the carefree business of riding the MV the 250 Honda really made me sit up. I managed to win the Japanese Grand Prix on it and

Honda promised me they would straighten out the snags. Later they lowered it, strengthened the frame and did their best to stop it bending in the middle.

'After that win, Honda asked me if I'd like to join the team. Jim, Ralph Bryans and Luigi Taveri hadn't been re-signed at this stage. Mr Sekiguchi whisked me off to the New Otani hotel, the biggest in Tokyo, and we spent a long time talking about what was wrong with the bikes and what could be done to improve them.

'There was no haggling over the cash. They agreed to the figure I suggested and I got precisely what I wanted. Three days after the race I signed the contract, without even dreaming I was going to be sticking my neck out as I'd never done before.

'Nobody at the factory knew just how bad the 500 was, because nobody there had ridden it anywhere near as fast, or under the same conditions, as I had to ride it. They had a test rider—a good man and a fair racer in Japan—and he took it out just the once. He came back after a quick spin and said it was perfect. Then he left the factory to go and work somewhere else. He wasn't so bloody daft! They never saw him again.

'Compared with the Honda, the MV was docile. There's no real knack of curbing the Honda's antics. Sometimes you can wind it on a bit more when it starts to play up and that will cure it; at other times that will make it worse. It was a case of trial and error; I had no idea what to do for the best.

'Look at my forearms. No wonder they're so big. I've been getting in a lot of weightlifting while I've been riding the Honda.

'When I first tried out the 500, in Japan at Christmas 1965, Honda agreed to cobble up a new frame. I went back three months later to try it out, and it wasn't much better. But we figured it had so much horsepower that nothing would get anywhere near it, and, having the legs of the other bikes, it should get through the season quite successfully.

'Anyway, my feeling later was that *I* wasn't going to ride it. Jim was. He'd made up his mind that he wanted the 500 title, even though I'd been signed by Honda to race the big bike. Jim got his way, and I was asked to concentrate on the 250 and 350 championships. None of us at Honda thought that anybody would come up with anything to beat the 500, however badly it handled. And if Count Agusta had marked time and made no improvements to the MV it would have walked the world championships.

'But when the new MV was introduced it was only about two miles an hour slower than the Honda—and a far better handler. The old MV had been something like twenty-five horse-power down on the Honda's ninety-plus.

'The fact that the Count wasn't caught napping was to some extent Honda's own fault; they'd been splashing it around all winter that they were going to unveil a hundred-horse-power 500. The Count knew what to expect and he got to work to combat Honda's plans. He concluded that my joining the Japanese outfit was the final proof.

'Honda built a 450 cc machine—a blown 350—that Jim Redman was going to ride in the Senior TT, the year before they had a full-out attempt for the 500 cc championships. It was entered for the race, with typical Honda secrecy, under the cover of the Rhodesian Motor-Cycle Club as Jim's private entry. Then Honda changed their minds and didn't go through with it, because they were afraid it would get blown off. But they were so anxious to win the 500 cc crown—it's still the one to have—that they got working on the full 500/four.

'I am sure they were so convinced that there would be no other bike fast enough to challenge it that they didn't put enough thought into it.'

Mike is in the unique position of having raced for both the world's top two big-bike factories. His experiences on the Honda and on the MV have left him with no doubt in his mind as to which bike he would prefer to ride in the bigger class.

The fact is that the MV has more good points and fewer bad ones than the Honda. And as for Mike's feelings with regard to the safety angle, he has had far fewer narrow escapes with the MV than with the Honda.

He certainly wasn't riding any slower in his MV days. In 1963 he went through the whole season breaking every lap- and race-record but one on the Grand Prix calendar. His one failure was in the Dutch TT when a rag was sucked into the carbs and he was put out of the running.

A look of inner contentment comes into his eyes whenever he talks about the MV. It is the same look that appears whenever the MV is drawn up against the Honda on the grid. It is the look that says, 'If only I could swop places for this race . . .'

The final judgement on the attractiveness of a motor-bike as a racing partner is based on its willingness to get round the hardest trial of all, the TT, without faltering in its stride. It is Mike's opinion that the MV fills the bill admirably (although, ironically, he won the 1967 Senior TT because the MV broke down).

'The MV is ideal for the TT and, consequently, for every Grand Prix. It has the ability to climb quickly over the mountain, superb acceleration and the right amount of speed, and it handles beautifully. The Norton probably comes closest behind it on most points, except speed. The MV has everything: it's the finest all-round machine I've ever ridden. At the Belgian Grand Prix in '65 it was doing more than 160 m.p.h. on about ten-five, ten-eight revs.

'One thing about the MV though, unlike the Honda, is that you daren't over-rev it. It wouldn't take it—it'd fall apart. The valves would bend and the pistons would blow. I never had to over-rev it, but Alan Shepherd did, two or three times, and it stopped on him. I suppose if you didn't have your eyes glued on the rev-counter, it would be easy to take it over the top. But when that needle gets up to around ten-eight, that's when you have to ease off. Ten-eight is the definite stop-mark—anything more, even 500 revs, and the engine would blow up. It's finicky that way.

'On the other hand you could miss a few gears occasionally and it would stand up to it. It burned a lot of oil, especially at the TT and because of this I had an extra oil-tank fitted under the saddle. I used to switch it on half-way through the race so it wasn't much of a problem to me.

'In four years of really hard riding the MV broke down on me only twice. At the Dutch in 1963 the mechanics left a rag in the carburettor, and when I was practising it got sucked in. It jammed the throttle slide wide open, and of course it revved like mad for about thirty seconds until I managed to shut off the carb with my hand. The mechanics didn't change the engine, and in the race I only went for one lap before the engine packed up. The second time it broke down was in Italy, during the pre-season warm-ups. I had to quit after valve trouble at San Remo.

'The only criticism I had of the MV's handling was that in flicking from, say, right to left, in very quick sections, you couldn't lift it up and put it down too easily. It was so heavy, the centrifugal force seemed to throw it out. I had to pull against it and it made the job particularly difficult.

'The more power you have at hand, the more delicate and sensitive your throttle control has to be. If you shut off a Norton the engine slows the bike down. But if you shut off an MV or a Honda the bike still goes flying on; you can't use the engine as a brake. That's where life on the multi-cylinder machines starts to get complicated.

'The MV has to be set up for a corner; the power has to be kept flowing on smoothly and easily all the way through. If you shut off the bike gets thrown out of its proper attitude, the back steps out and you're in danger of being unloaded.

'It's probably the heaviest bike I've ridden, and on bumpy sections that's something of a boon. It really sticks close to the road, though you have to be wary of screwing the power on too heftily because there is so much of it. If you're a bit ham-fisted, the thrust, like the Honda's, is so fearsome that the wheels spin like mad and the back end tries to come round. Handled properly the power will push you along like a rocket; but you can't afford to be over-anxious, especially away from the start or when you're exiting from a corner.

'The first time I rode the MV I was completely taken by it. I spent a whole day with one at Monza, and after a few laps testing it I was getting round only a second or two outside the lap record. Then I won my first race on it when Gary Hocking had to retire in the Italian.

'The MV was a masterpiece of machinery, a racing thoroughbred. Do you know I could lean it over at fifty-nine degrees from the vertical? Dunlop's ran a test at the Dutch.

'I never had to worry about the bike; I could put it through corners almost as fast as I liked and it wouldn't veer off its path. I couldn't do that with the Honda. The centre of gravity is too high, much higher than the MVs. The Honda is top-heavy, too high off the road. I don't known why the Japanese make their machines like this—the Yamahas are the same. Oddly enough, though, despite its top-heaviness, the 500 Honda isn't more readily laid over. I don't know why; it seems to defy the law of balance.'

How did Mike feel about those two tough seasons, 1966 and 1967, when he had made the move from MV?

'I would say that riding ability counted throughout those two seasons more than for a long time. I had to ride as I'd never done before to give the big Honda any chance at all against the MV.

'I chanced much more than I dared hope to get away with. Remember, I knew exactly what the MV and Agostini could do; and I would say the advantage was theirs. I'm not knocking Ago and I'm not praising the MV any more than it deserves, nor am I overstating the bad handling of the Honda.

'I can't imagine there is a spectator anywhere in the world who has watched Ago and me racing and felt he hasn't had good return for his entry money. The racing between us has been really hard and uncompromising. Each Grand Prix has been fought out on the basis of sheer riding ability, except when one of us has had to pull out because of mechanical failure.'

My view is that when Mike was matched against Agostini, probably the most brilliant and consistent of all the Italian aces, the tension before the race was plain to see among the crowds. Each event was a sure success; nobody stayed in the bars or slept in the long grass when these two were fighting for championship points.

Honda, in deference to their veteran servant Jim Redman's wish to win the 500 cc championship, allowed the Rhodesian the best bikes in that class. Mike, who had almost made the title his own property with his four successive championships on the MV, was not entirely pleased. Mike had been signed ostensibly to ride the 500, and now it was Redman who was bidding for the championship. Honda, appreciative of the fine service given to them by Redman, made no move to alter the situation; and Mike had to be content with second best. He became Redman's support rider in the class he himself most wanted to win.

Then, half-way through the 1966 season, Jim retired from racing, his arm almost paralysed after a heavy spill at 120 m.p.h. in the pouring rain at the Belgian Grand Prix. The arm refused to mend quickly enough, and he was forced out of the running for the 500 championship and, later, out of racing.

This left Mike in a terrible fix. Already deeply involved in the 250 and 350 classes, he now had to take over where Jim had left off and try to get on terms with Agostini. It was virtually an impossible task. He made a monumental effort, but he was forced to chase a man who was riding superbly and who had built up a massive lead on points. The turning-point of the championship came at the Italian Grand Prix. Mike, piling it on magnificently, closed on Agostini, but his valves buckled—they were faulty. It put him out of the race and left Agostini with a clear run home. So Mike, who had clinched the 250 and 350 titles, only missed the hat-trick by the slenderest of margins.

In 1967 he again took the 250 and 350 titles—but the 500 cc race, once more at its most vital stage, finished catastrophically for him. He had opened up a seventeen-second lead with only two laps left when the crankshaft, which had been put in only a few thousandths of an inch out of true, buckled. Agostini, once again in luck, swept past the Honda, stuck in top gear, in front of a grandstand full of Italians who were literally weeping with joy.

Mike, bitterly disappointed, pulled in at the end of the pit straight and pushed the Honda roughly against a wall. He strode off, close to tears, shouldering his way through the pack of Japanese mechanics who had scampered to see what was wrong. He refused to take his place on the winner's rostrum until persuaded to by Bill Ivy. When he did, Agostini pulled him up onto the number-one step, which indicated the Italian's own particular feelings about the result.

'I was about three minutes from winning that race,' said Mike. 'Three minutes, that's all, and a stupid thing like that had to go wrong. I could have cried.

'It was the last of the European classics and I needed to win there to have a chance of taking the championship in Canada. If there'd been a river near enough I'd have thrown the Honda into it, I was that sick of it. There was all hell to pay for the mechanic who had prepared the bike.

'The cumulative effect of a long hard season—my toughest ever—and the disappointment of losing at Monza were just too much for me. I'd been doing the work of three riders. I needed somebody to support me, to take a bit of the weight off my shoulders. I'd carried the full responsibility for all three classes. Ralph Bryans tried hard enough on the 250, but he wasn't too happy about it. He's essentially a 125 and 50 cc man. I needed somebody who could beat Phil Read and Bill Ivy, or at least somebody who would give them something to worry about. As it was it was two-to-one against me, and I had the slower bike in the 250 class.

'I looked around and checked one or two riders, but I couldn't find anybody who was competitive enough to do what I needed. The general standard of riding was quite low. I know that may sound a harsh comment on the racing scene, but it's true. There were plenty of good average riders, but nobody who stood out as anything exceptional.

'Another man could have taken care of one class for me—though I don't know which, they were all heavy going. Maybe we could have sat somebody on the 350 and he'd have won, but it was a thin hope. Certainly those riders who were around when we were looking for somebody to help couldn't have matched Read, Ivy or Agostini.

'Honda seemed quite content to leave it all to me; they seemed to assume that as I was winning a few races there was no absolute necessity to engage anyone else. It was a good economic proposition for them—they were getting three men's work for one man's pay.

'Anyway, the problem resolved itself in February 1968. Without any prior warning, Honda decided to quit motor-bike racing. When I was suddenly summoned to Japan, I thought it was to test the season's new bikes. It came as a terrible shock when I found out the real reason: I was out of a job.

'Mr Sekiguchi took me out to dinner and told me that the factory wanted to spend more time and money on the development of the Formula One car, because they were going into the commercial car market in a really big way. It must have been a quickly taken decision, because the factory had made a new 250 and had almost finished a 350 and a 500 in preparation for the 1968 season.

'It was obviously too late for me to get a job anywhere else, as all the other works teams had settled their plans and their budgets for the coming season. Mr Sekiguchi offered to pay me not to ride any other products, and the money was so tempting that I signed a contract to that effect. He promised me a 250, a 350 and a 500—the 1967 models—to race at national and international meetings, but on the understanding that I didn't enter them for the classics. The alternative, he pointed out, was a smaller sum of money as settlement and freedom to ride where and what I wanted. But the money, as I said, was too good to turn down.

'I looked on it as a good chance to wind up my career. It's my intention to quit racing at the end of '68, and to be paid not to ride in the world championships was an attractive offer!

'But I was still awfully disappointed at Honda's decision to abandon racing. I badly wanted to finish up with the 500 cc championship, when I'd missed it twice by such very narrow margins. I also wanted to set up a record of world championship wins; now I'll have to share that privilege with Ubbiali, who, like me, scored nine.

'The Honda decision demonstrates, I think, that business always comes first with them. They'd won just about everything possible, and had tried two years running to clinch the only championship they couldn't win, the 500. They obviously felt they were wasting their time and money when the cash could be better spent on a commercial project.

'They showed the same attitude in their dealings with me: for example, if I was ever prevented from racing in a Grand Prix because of an injury at a non-classic meeting, it was written into my contract that I would have had to repay them £700 for each championship event I missed.

'I can't imagine they'll take too long to get John Surtees's Grand Prix car scoring successfully, just as they did when they first moved into the motor-bike-racing business.'

8 The Car Game

When Mike almost blithely decided that he would like to try his hand at car racing, following in the steps of John Surtees, he didn't fully appreciate the problems he was letting himself in for. Nor did he realize that he was entering what was to be the unhappiest phase of his racing life. Where he had expected success he found only disappointment and frustration, and the experience taught him a bitter lesson that he cannot forget. He left motor racing a saddened man, chastened by his lack of success and smarting at his failure to make an impact.

We talked for many long hours of the disappointments he experienced, his feelings while he was racing, the differences between motorcycle and motor-car racing and the attitude of the people who hovered inside the four-wheel world.

He describes the venture with rancour and a feeling of bitterness.

'When I decided to go into motor racing I made the biggest mistake of my life. I was twenty-three, and I thought the time was ripe for me to make the switch from bikes to cars. I was going to show the world what I could do; I was going to prove that my skills weren't limited to performances on two wheels. Cars, I thought, would be a pushover, and it never occurred to me that it wouldn't be simple to make the change. I was convinced I could do it with reasonable success, otherwise I would never have made the move.

'The entire two-and-a-half-year period I had in cars had me alternately soaring in hope and plunging to the depths of despair and disappointment. I made about as much impression as I would have done if I'd decided to become a world champion tennis-player. Successes were rare and failures seemed to be waiting round every corner. When I made up my mind that I'd had enough and removed myself from the scene I was a very bewildered young man. Worst of all my pride was severely dented, and there was no escape from that awful feeling.

'It's not easy for a man who is a champion in one world to accept that he cannot be champion in another one of his own choice. Nobody forced me to go car racing; I'd had a few offers, but the final decision was my own. I thought I was adequately equipped to carry it through.

'But I went about the whole enterprise in the wrong way; my attitudes were wrong for a start. I wanted to run before I could walk, in what is a highly competitive business. I didn't appreciate that being the tops in one business means exactly nothing in another; reputations scare nobody in motor-car racing. It's how good you are on the day, how efficient your machinery is, that counts.

'The more involved I became in the car business, the more it came home to me that I was right down there at the bottom, an apprentice, and a raw one at that, in the company of experts. I was only playing the game; they were in it to make it pay in a hardened professional manner.

'I had to learn a completely different set of techniques, a different approach, with vastly varying mechanical hazards to master. I was almost dizzy trying to unravel the mysteries of how to set up and prepare a car for racing. My overall impression, looking back on those days, is that you need as much technical and mechanical knowledge as skill to race a car. And my non-technical brain couldn't cope, it couldn't absorb quickly enough all the ponderous ins-and-outs vital to the smooth, accurate running of a capricious motor-car.

'Not only was I in a strange new world, I was faced with an utterly different language as well. The conversations in the pits were unintelligible to me. They were a stream of phrases I'd hardly ever heard before, words that I couldn't understand. There were problems of toe-in and toe-out; camber, castor, roll-centres, wet tyres, dry tyres and Lord knew what else. I was expected to master all of these problems, when all I wanted to do was cram myself into the cockpit and get down to the racing.

'These technicalities left me both bored and bemused; first, because I didn't know what they meant; and, secondly, because when I tried to understand they became no clearer.

'Even though it was vitally necessary to sort out all this stuff to get the car running without it slopping about all over the track, I had to fumble along in the dark. I used the dunce's principle of trial and error, and unfortunately for me it turned out to be mostly error. It just made me even more frustrated.

'I began to realize that races were won as much on effort in the paddock and pits as they were on the circuit. The flutter of the flag to start a race was merely the beginning of an extension to what had been going on in the paddock in the previous days.

'With the wrong toe-in or toe-out, the car veered wildly from side to side and was virtually impossible to handle with any safety. It used to take me two or three hours' training merely to sort out these 'minor' problems. Then, having got the car in some sort of order, I had to concentrate on getting round the circuit in a decent time, against the world's best drivers, often in a car that was still unstable despite all my struggles. I must have been a hair-raising sight to some of the more experienced drivers.

'The troubles I was having must have been obvious to the others, because they were constantly offering me help. The snag was that I *knew* what was wrong with the car. I knew the feel and the balance were wrong somewhere—but I couldn't explain the trouble. It was frustrating knowing that the car wasn't right but not being able to do anything about it other than complain.

'Short of driving the car themselves, which of course was out of the question, the other drivers could get no idea of what I was talking about and when I tried to explain I got tongue-tied. Consequently, I was too often struggling to compensate with my driving for the car's erratic behaviour.

'I'm well aware that every driver has to go through all this at some time; and I know that it would all have come clear to me eventually. I understand, too, that disappointment in car racing may stem from over-anxiety and lack of experience; but I was desperate to do well, and to do well quickly. I was down-hearted because, hard as I strove, I couldn't achieve any measure of success.

'I must have covered miles in the paddock, running about looking for somebody to help me out of my dilemmas. Graham Hill was my chief target. I never left him alone, but he was as patient and understanding as always. I can't remember a time when he showed even the slightest resentment. He's one of my happier memories of motor racing.

'Over the years Graham has jotted all the problems he has encountered into a little black notebook. When he goes to a circuit he simply flips the pages and finds out what problems to expect and how the car should be set up to beat them; this way his motors are always in perfect order.

'Each time I approached him with my troubles he used to thumb through the book and ask, "Do you think this is what's wrong? Or is it that?" He would, in his unruffled way, go through the book until I thought I recognized the ailment. Too often, however, the rules for his car didn't apply to mine.

'But there was a lot more behind my flop in car racing than just the baffling technical setbacks. Many people, I know, have since laughed up their sleeves because I didn't have the triumph I would have liked.

'I suppose there are always know-alls around to say, "Well, old son, I did tell you, you know." They get some sort of pleasure out of the accuracy of their forecasts. And that was just the sort of response I didn't want. I'm afraid that those who were unwise enough to pass remarks received some cutting replies.

'It's one thing to realize you've made a mistake, and another to be regularly reminded of it. Patience, in the light of such arrant and stupid advice, is not one of my strong points. I fully realized my own mistakes, without any outsiders having to emphasize them.

'I certainly don't want to make any excuses for my failure in cars—but there were *reasons*.

'I'd hovered on the brink of a switch from two wheels to four for ages; I'd secretly nursed the ambition to change without really making an attempt to do anything about it. For a long time I was in a muddle of advice. There were people who said, "Have a go." There were others who advised, "Stay where you are, on bikes." And there were more who said that they thought I could mix the two.

'I'd had a tiny taste, enough to whet my appetite for car racing, one wet, cold and windy morning at Silverstone in 1960.

'The UDT Laystall team was there; Ken Gregory and a couple of drivers. They invited me along for a try-out to see if I would be of any use to them. I was flattered by the offer.

'I'd never even sat in a racing car before. I used to rush round in my own 3·8 Jaguar, but of course there was a world of difference, and the margin soon dawned on me.

'I was loosed off in a Lotus 4 Climax. The idea, it seemed, was to throw me in at the deep end to see if I came up again. I had no sensation of danger, no worries. I had no idea that in the rain—and there was plenty of it about—these cars can be extremely dodgy.

'After a lap or two I began to get the feel of the Lotus, to get the hang of its power. My confidence welled up and I decided that I'd try to get round Maggot's Corner flat out. The fact that the rain was bouncing about a foot high off the track didn't worry me. The road was wet and shiny as a mirror, but I was in a mood of sheer delight, bordering on hysteria. I was like a kid with a new toy. But the Lotus was anything but that.

'I steered towards Maggot's yelling "Whoopee!" foot pressed hard to the floor and totally unaware of the threat of any danger. I was hard into the bend when I lost control completely, the car ran away with me and clouted the banking with considerable force.

'Whatever cockiness I had in me was knocked out there and then. A great scarlet blush took the place of the excited look on my face as I motored, with a good deal of embarrassment, back towards the pits in the bent and battered car.

'They were quite kind to me, really. I think they'd half expected this to happen, just from watching me going round the circuit. Nobody rebuked me, there was no criticism, at least not while I was still there. They said they'd let me know, and I'm still waiting. . . .

'Before I'd spun off I'd just managed to get round at two minutes for the lap. Innes Ireland had been lapping steadily, without any apparent effort, at something like one minute fifty-three.

'Some bloke at the pits had spent a great deal of time dashing from shelter to hang out signals to me. My answer was to keep skimming his toes without seeing what was chalked on the board. In the end he threw down the board in disgust and walked off. I suppose he reckoned I wasn't taking too much notice; he was trying to warn me about the slippery conditions.

'I gave up the idea of car racing there and then, and decided I was best fitted to motor-cycle racing. These were early days for me in bike racing and, up to then, I hadn't won a championship.

'The bug to race cars didn't bite me again until 1962. Then, I thought, I was a little older, a little wiser and more ready to have another try. I was fairly well established on the motor-cycle race scene, but even so I was anxious to move over to cars. I thought about it, argued about it, and decided that the only way I could find out if I would be any good was to have a go.

'I scratched my name on a cheque for £1,700 and bought a Formula Junior Brabham. Then I went shopping for a sky blue driver's suit, a pair of lightweight shoes and a large helmet . . . and went racing.

'I drove my Dodge shooting-brake and trailer down to Weybridge to collect the car from Brabham's place. I'd entered myself at Brands Hatch for the following day. The car wasn't ready when I called for it, and I had to wait until 11 p.m. before I could pick it up. But, when I saw it being wheeled out, the waiting seemed worthwhile. The yellow paint gleamed and the Cosworth–Ford engine crackled crisply enough to make me tingle. The mechanics wished me luck and I set off for Brands—and my car-racing début.

'I didn't get to Brands until the early hours of the morning. I slept in the back of the Dodge, but I was so nervous I don't think I got more than an hour's sleep all night. Everybody expected me to do well.

'The car was brand, spanking new, and had never been run. When I took it out for training I was delighted to discover that it would top 108 m.p.h. I finished up with a good placing on the grid, and the world that morning seemed a much rosier place.

'It was like coming home, racing at Brands. The circuit was as familiar to me as my own garden. The atmosphere, too, made me feel at home. All that was missing were the faces of motor-cycle riders. Instead I was surrounded by people I didn't know. This made it a new world to me. The flags, the crowds, the smell of high-octane fuel and the paddock were familiar, but that was where the similarity ended.

'In this, my first race, I had to chase a man who later became famous outside motor racing. His name was Roy James, now in jail for his part in the Great Train Robbery. I certainly wouldn't envy anybody who had to catch him. I tried hard but all I ever saw was the disappearing tail-end of his car.

'Roy James won and I managed fifth place. James was a fine driver, and, but for his other vocation, could probably have done extremely well in the car-racing business.

'I was quite pleased with my first attempt—and I was delighted with the Brabham, it was a flyer. I painted its nose black and had a black line daubed up the centre of the yellow front. At least, I thought, I'd be noticed, however far back in the field I might finish; even if I couldn't win the spectators would know I'd turned up for the meeting.

'I took the Brabham to as many meetings as I could fit in between my commitments on motor-bikes. At my second outing I managed to win, then followed it up with three more victories.

'By this time I imagined I was ready for the big stuff, the Grand Prix scene. My confidence had increased, and I'd served a reasonable period of apprenticeship in the Junior ranks.

'Reg Parnell, an old friend of Stan's from pre-war racing days, had been trying for a long time to persuade me to make the break from bikes and change over to cars. He had been team manager for Bowmaker, and when they pulled out of racing he took over the cars, a Lotus 24 with a V8 Climax engine, and two V8-engined Lolas, both with Climaxes.

'I'd been putting Reg off for months, but when he asked me once

At Clermont Ferrand, showing how to lean to the limit.

John Hartle, in Mike's view one of the finest-ever riders, steers the Gilera round the Ulster Grand Prix circuit at Dundrod.

After his TT spill Mike kicks the fairing of his MV back into position. Then, against all regulations, he pushed off down hill, into the flow of traffic, to get the machine started.

After the 500 cc Czechoslovakian Grand Prix at Brno with (*left*) Agostini, and John Cooper.

The structural differences that marked the discrepancies in behaviour between the 500 cc Honda and the big MV.

Mike and Jim Redman, the Honda team captain, discuss tactics.

How not to win races . . .

Top: Parting company with a 250 Benelli at Monza, 1962.

Middle: Leaving the MV at Modena in 1964.

Lower: Leading on the last corner of the last lap at Brands Hatch in 1963.

more I agreed. I was flushed with the success I'd had with the Formula Junior and felt ready to make my name in cars.

'It took a great deal of heart-searching and critical self-investigation, but I concluded that there was little left for me on bikes. I'd achieved most of the things I wanted—the world one-hour championship was mine after a trip to Daytona, I had won world titles and scored TT wins.

'I decided not to break completely, however, at least not until I was established and could make enough money to live on as I had done with motor-bikes. I opted to mix both sports; I was making plenty of money with MV and I realized it would be foolish to throw it all over to enter for Grand Prix car racing as a private runner. I was hoping to do well enough in cars to be picked up by one of the works outfits; if that had happened, I would have stopped racing bikes altogether.

'The Count had no objections to my racing cars, provided it didn't interfere with the world motor-cycle championship programme. One of the contracts he offered me every year was one to drive an MV car. He always said that one day he would build one and he would expect me to drive it for him. It never existed, not even on the drawing-board so far as I knew, but he still used to pay me £2,500 a year to drive it. I certainly wasn't going to turn down money for nothing; it's the easiest cash I ever earned.

'After discussions with Reg Parnell I bought a half-share in his Formula One team and partnered Chris Amon. I thought this was the best way to go racing, the quickest way to be spotted by a works-team manager.

'Reg, who knew motor racing inside out, was able to pass on a good many tips, and was able to give me more help than I could have got from anybody else. He taught me a few tricks of this very new trade, but it was clear to me that Formula One racing isn't the sort of sport that you can master overnight; you have to have years of experience to be fully versed in all its intricate arts.

'The team went to Silverstone—again!—for tests. I'm convinced I saw the track staff belting for cover when they recognized me as the lunatic who had scattered them all two years before.

'I was as much on trial as the Lotus we took there. Reg stared out from the pits watching my progress through his keen, critical eyes; he could see faults that I couldn't hope to notice. After a few practice laps he said he was pleased with my performance, and told me, "Considering the car and your inexperience you did well, but there's a lot of room for improvement. You've a lot to learn."

'I don't think that even Reg realized quite how much there was for me to learn.

'I tempered my tests with a fair amount of caution, in the light of the memory of the hairy outing I'd had on the same track two years earlier. There was, of course, the financial consideration, too. I owned a half-share and I wasn't too anxious to risk bending the equipment when I knew it was going to cost me money to put it right again.

'The arrangement I entered with Reg was as much a business one as a plan to learn how to race among the big boys of Grand Prix events. I couldn't hope to make any big money out of it; I assumed that my principal value to the team was the publicity they would get from my joining them. For my own purposes and ambitions it meant that I had my own training-ground, cars that were half mine. I wasn't responsible to anybody else for the machinery. Chris Amon was a salaried driver, but I was employed as a driver without wages; I was to take a part share of the profits. All I got were expenses and—this was a laugh—prize-money. The trouble was, there wasn't a lot of that knocking about.

'After a while, when we found we weren't having any success worth talking about, we decided to invest in equipment that might give us the breakthrough. We bought a Lotus that Jim Clark had been using for two seasons, the car he'd been driving when he won the world championship. Originally it had been fitted with a Climax engine, but Reg thought it would be more economical to stick a BRM unit in. He argued that it would be much cheaper to maintain and would help cut down the running costs by a great margin.

'When we collected the shell from Colin Chapman, he told us that if we did put a BRM engine in it the car would never go; he explained that the car had been designed for Climax torque and weight. He said a BRM engine couldn't possibly send it along as well as the car could go. However, Reg had his way, I bowed to his superior experience and knowledge, and we put the BRM unit into the Lotus.

'As it turned out, Chapman's words of advice were painfully prophetic. The car never seemed to go right. The main trouble stemmed from the engine; then we had trouble with the five-speed gear-box, a new one, and, as if that wasn't enough to worry us, the car wouldn't handle properly.

'We seemed to go through an engine a meeting, and it began to cost us a pile of money. One bill alone, from BRM, set us back £8,000 for a season's racing. It was a season of only a dozen races, too, with very little to show for it. I picked up a championship point for a sixth place at Monaco and Chris collected two or three points, including a fifth at the Dutch.

'Clearly this was business lunacy, and something had to be done. My motor-cycle winnings were subsidizing my interest in the car team. I was like two different men—in the bike world I was having great success and loving every minute, in the car business I was getting nowhere and was as miserable as sin.

'I began to realize I'd blundered and was wasting not only my time but my money into the bargain. The returns, in all aspects, were precisely nil.

'We couldn't finish a race. All the other drivers were flashing by, while we sat at the side of the track in a broken car wondering what had gone wrong now. Unaccountably the engines blew up at almost every meeting, and they spent more time at the BRM factory than they did in the cars. I began to wonder and worry whether it was my fault, whether I was working them too hard trying to keep up with the others.

'I began to dread the car meetings. I always looked enviously at the works drivers who had only to jump into the cars and steer them, and compared their position with mine, where the only thing that went was my money.

'It's probably just as well we didn't have the Climax engines, because, with our luck, the bills would have been doubled, I didn't make a penny out of the team: it ran itself with the takings from start money, oil contracts, bonuses and other sponsorships. It's a puzzle to me how any private teams can make money from racing. Rob Walker, with Stirling Moss and Bonnier, seems to be the sole exception.

'We were really up against it trying to match the big companies like Ferrari, Lotus and Brabham, with their superbly professional drivers and big money support. We never stood a chance; we were trying to lick them with hack equipment that was about as useful as a clothes-horse in the Grand National.

'I had the occasional enjoyable race, but more often than not I was right down in the dumps, a spectator in a race, watching the other boys steaming by and helpless to do anything about it. Every race added something more to shatter my dreams and, when I should have been getting great fun out of handling a high-speed motor in the hurly-burly of Grand Prix racing, I was being pushed, slowly but ever so surely, towards retirement.

'It didn't make it any the more enjoyable when I raced cars at circuits like Spa, in Belgium, where I'd raced motor-bikes in the past. There must have been thousands of people in the crowds who had watched me race bikes, seen me win and break a record, and expected me to do the same thing in a car. It was odd to be in that situation, to be fêted one week and a week later to be an unnoticed no-hoper. I couldn't get used to it.

'One advantage I did have in racing on circuits that I knew was that I didn't have to waste any time learning my way round. I had more time to try to get round at a good pace for a favourable position on the grid. I wasn't having to do two things, as the others were—learn the circuit and get used to the car. Once or twice, on a circuit I knew really well, I could get round in training quicker than some of the star drivers. I'd earn myself a good place on the grid only to be let down by the car during the race itself.

'One of the best positions I had, because I knew so much about the circuit, was in the Austrian Grand Prix in 1964. Half-way through the race I was fourth, and holding it quite comfortably. There was a string of bigger-name drivers behind me.

'Then something—I don't know what, naturally—fell off the car and I dropped back to eighth place. The bad luck was arriving in large doses and it didn't stop there. The same year, at the United States GP, I strove really hard to work my way into fourth place. Everything, it seemed, was at last going smoothly There were no groans from the engine and I was an easy fourth. Six laps from the finish I noticed the oil-pressure needle whizzing down to the zero mark, and taking my hopes with it. The oil-pipe had blown off, and the stuff smothered me and everybody else around. There was such a short distance to go that I decided to stick it out and try to finish, but half a lap later the car decided it had suffered long enough and stopped. It was the second time, in extremely competitive company, that I had managed to get myself well placed only to be let down by the car.

'I'm sure nobody could have blamed me for feeling bitter at being robbed of the chance to show I wasn't the clown a lot of people thought I was.

'Even when I picked up my one and only championship point, at Monaco, the car was handling with mulish awkwardness, and this of course harked back to my lack of knowledge in setting it up. I'd never run the car with topped-up fuel-tanks—I'd put in only enough to see me through the practice sessions.

'In the race we filled up with petrol and this naturally added to the weight. The result was monstrous oversteer, and I spent most of the race wrestling with the steering, yanking and forcing it to go round the corners, until my wrists were numbed with the effort. It had to happen on a circuit where sheer driving skill, and not power, is the essential factor.

'If I'd realized that this simple problem could be so much of a hazard I might have been able to work myself into a much higher place. But, as so often before, I'd fallen once again into the trap of technicalities; it was nobody's fault but my own.

'I lost heart almost completely in 1964. There was still plenty of fight left in me, but none in my cars. Then, to top it all, Reg died. I had lost a good friend and valuable collaborator. His son, Tim, took over, but I missed all those words of wisdom, the advice and non-stop encouragement that had helped to make everything so much brighter when the chips were down.

'I was getting weary of the tiresome travelling I was forced to undertake in order to cover as many bike and car meetings as possible. Then I found that I was having less time to myself because I was concentrating so hard on both the sports. To concentrate wholly on one pursuit is wearing enough, but to cover two major sports adequately is utterly exhausting.

'In 1964, for instance, I'd had a hard period in the Isle of Man, training and racing at the TT. The following week I went to Holland for the Dutch TT at Assen. The races there were run on a Saturday, and I'd entered for a car meeting at Rouen on Sunday. I practised for the Dutch then rushed off to Rouen for training in the cars.

'On the Friday night before the motor-cycle races I tried to get back from Rouen to Assen, but the weather was so bad that the aircraft I had chartered was held up. We were grounded at Rouen for ages. After a few hours we did get away and I had to snatch some sleep as we flew to Holland. I arrived at the circuit just in time for the first race, which I managed to win. Then I had to hang about at the circuit waiting for my next race, which was the last one on the programme.

'After winning it—it was the 500 cc race, a really gruelling one in almost tropical heat—I braked the bike as hard as I could just after the finishing-line and handed it over to my mechanic. My car was parked alongside the circuit, just by the exit. Still in my leathers I ran over to it to get on my way without wasting a second; I didn't even have time to wait for the garlanding ceremony. I had to get to Rouen and I couldn't afford to hang about for a moment longer than necessary. I had to drive throughout the night to Rouen for the Sunday car race. After three hundred and fifty miles or so of driving in the dark, then racing at Rouen, I was just about on my last legs.

'The rot really began to set in during the 1965 season. I went to Sicily but, sickeningly, the engine blew up again when I was eighth fastest in practice. It was the second year running I'd had trouble there. In 1964 I spun off into a lake at around 130 m.p.h. It wasn't the crash that worried me so much; the lake was full of snakes and I was up to my neck in them. I went for the shore like a torpedo.

'Dickie Attwood, the BRM third-string driver, joined our outfit whenever his team didn't have a car for him. When he came over the BRM factory agreed to allow him to use a works engine. We put the works engine in my car for the Syracuse race, and when I tried it out I could scarcely believe the difference. The car was streets faster than it had ever been before. For once the spectators were able to notice the dark blue and red Lotus 25 not so much for its failure as for its surprising zest.

'In the race I had a titanic dice with Bonnier for fourth place and, at last, I was enjoying every minute. The car was behaving itself and going like a dream. Then, when I was heading into a quick corner, an ignition pick-up wire fell off and the car went into a big slide. I went off the road and out of the race with a lifeless motor. Just when everything had seemed to be going swimmingly I was left cursing my rotten luck.

'From there I went to Monaco and had to scratch really hard to qualify. Things were getting on top of me. I couldn't hide my frustration and anger at the dreadful series of setbacks that never seemed to let up. Tim Parnell flew to Monaco to watch the race, and saw me pull out with gear-box trouble ten laps after the start; it was the last straw. I decided there and then to quit altogether. I'd had enough; I felt that I couldn't take any more disappointments. I told Tim that I was fed up to the teeth with the whole business and that I wanted to sell out my share of the team. Chris Amon had already left to join Bruce McLaren.

'Chris's record, by the way, is part of the proof that we might have done better with machinery that was a little more reliable. Since he left the team he hasn't looked back and he's shown what a great driver he is.

'Anyway, Tim agreed to my suggestion and I got back most of the money I'd put in. I reasoned that I also gained a lot of experience that I could well have done without.

'At this stage I was setting off to go to races knowing in my heart that I wouldn't be able to finish in them, and that's no way to go racing. Under conditions like that anybody with his heart set on winning would have felt precisely the same.

'The only way a private driver can do well in GP racing is if all the works teams break down; and driving under those conditions, more in hope than with efficiency, is a silly ambition. I certainly didn't want to win merely because everybody else had been forced to pull out. I wanted to win by my own skill. Nothing else would have been satisfactory. The cold fact is that I couldn't even get placed.

'Even now, despite that bitter experience, I don't believe I failed because I wasn't competitive. I know I was; my positions before I broke down were proof enough to me. My cars simply weren't good enough, they were never a match for the works boys.

'The one definite aim I had in mind was to be recognized and signed by a works team. All my efforts were moulded to this end, but I think I ruined any chances I might have had by making a supreme mess of my brief excursion into four-wheel racing. I was foolish enough to hope that I could make a good show on clapped-out equipment. Without the proper tools it's impossible to do a reasonable job.

'The ironical aspect of it all is that in motor-cycle racing the situation was completely reversed. In that business I had the upper hand. I had the finest machinery, fussed over and cared for by works mechanics and backed by a millionaire's money and experience.

'If I hadn't been used to this style of treatment in my own business, I suppose the hardships of privateering in cars might not have hit me so hard.

'One of the things that annoyed me most of all about car racing was the tribe of hangers-on. There was a constant following of absolutely useless people who, it seemed to me, merely wanted to rub shoulders with the drivers in order to achieve some sort of status. Every driver I know is cursed by this particular breed of bore. It happens in motor-cycle racing too, but not nearly as much as in Formula One racing.

'I was never really accepted among the car-racing fraternity; I was made to feel very much an outsider because, I suppose, a motor-cycle racer isn't quite the sort of person one should be seen with. This vein of snobbishness seemed to run through the people who actually had nothing to do with the racing, the people not attached in a direct way to the business. They were the people who latched on to the teams, or the individual drivers, and offered nothing except boredom. The drivers were all fine, friendly blokes who were ready to help a beginner whenever they could spare the time. They had all been through what I was experiencing and they knew the difficulties and frustrations.

'Before I started racing cars I used to go to the meetings as a spectator. The hangers-on were always stopping me in the paddock to say hello and ask me when I was going to move over to cars.

'Then, when I did make the switch, and in doing so blundered badly, they all ignored me. You have to be a success to be "in" with these people. In my own world, which was outside theirs, everything was all right. But when I moved into their little sphere they didn't want to know me.

'I found that later they wouldn't even pass the time of day with me. To my mind that was a revealing illustration of their ill manners, contrary to their own ideas of good breeding.

'Being a racing motor-cyclist seemed to be something of a slur in the eyes of the hangers-on. Even after all this time in motor racing John Surtees is still tagged "former racing motor-cyclist". Bob Anderson was too, and he'd almost forgotten he'd ever raced bikes.

'It's as if they want you to be kept in your place and to make you remember that, after all, you are some sort of lesser being. They might as well tag you for a hobby, or a job, you did years ago. Something like "one-time darts champion of the Bull and Bush". In other words, the tag is useless information.

'The top drivers couldn't be snooty if they tried; that is apparently the prerogative of the people who have more money than brains and demonstrate it by the way they drive in order to impress their friends. With their string-back gloves, chequered stickers and club badges festooned all over their cars, their inane chatter about "shunts and prangs", they are only playing a game of racing.

'Conversely the professionals realize it's no game; they're earning a living in a fiercely competitive sport, and they appreciate that there is little fun and a lot of hard work in racing.

'The professional looks on his car not as a showpiece but as an instrument by which he earns his bread and butter. It's a deadly serious business, and a dangerous one, and they treat it as such. The fun comes after the race has finished.

'Many of the club-level racers look on a car as a status symbol, something sleek and shiny that crackles noisily but goes nowhere slowly. There are, of course, the other kind of club-racers, the good ones who are trying hard to burst out of the club scene into big-time racing. They get my admiration because they, at least, are really trying to be serious, not just pretending to be.

'I found that the motor-racing journalists were as bad as anybody else. On motor-bikes, even the no-hopers earn a good write-up if they've really tried and done better than usual. The same sympathy doesn't apply in car racing. You're either in the top bracket or you don't exist.

'This is the aspect of motor racing I found hardest to understand. I suppose it boils down to a personal thing; I was fussed over and fêted in the motor-bike world, but ignored to a large degree in cars.

'I noticed, too, that there was very little mixing between car drivers. The teams stuck closely together at their hotels and they were clannish in the extreme, unlike the rival motor-bike teams. It doesn't matter how fierce the rivalry is among motor-cycle racers, there is a great feeling of comradeship. At every meeting we all get together to talk about the race or to booze in one big party. Most times we stay in the same hotel unless we have our caravans with us—and the no-hopers are as welcome as the bigger stars.

'In the car circle I was very much on my own, on the fringe, often with only the rest of the team to keep me company. I found this pretty upsetting, because by nature I'm a gregarious type of man who enjoys mixing in with people to relax and have a good laugh.

'Surtees, I believe, had the same sort of trouble. But John's a different sort of character, and probably doesn't like company as much as I do. He hasn't spoken to me too often about the problems he had when he first started car racing, but I'm sure they were similar to the ones I had when I started. I know that we both share the feeling of the difference between car and motor-bike racing.

'Contrary to the widely held belief, I think that bikes are far more comfortable than Formula One cars. Fatigue, for one thing, is far less pronounced. Weariness comes more quickly in a racing-car.

'The techniques are quite different, too. The only common factor is speed; after that there's little resemblance between the two ways of getting round a circuit.

'Cars, naturally, are much faster, and they can be drifted through corners without losing too much speed. Bikes, on the other hand, have to be taken carefully round corners, without the tyres shifting off line.

'I found at Clermont-Ferrand, during the 1966 French Grand Prix, that I could get the 250 Honda six round the circuit in ten seconds less than the old lap record. I was really trying. But I discovered that even at my quickest I was still twelve seconds slower than a Formula One car's fastest lap. This is why any race between a car and a bike round the TT circuit would be farcical. The car would win every time.

'Most of the time spent in a car leaves the driver in some sort of agony or other. It's like a high-speed torture chamber. You find aches in muscles you never even knew existed. You rap your knuckles on the bits around the steering-wheel. Your feet get burned by the oil that bubbles and drips on your shoes, and your ankles ache from the non-stop work on the pedals.

'Neck muscles feel as if they've been pulled out of line; they get strained to the limit of endurance with the weight of the helmet and the effort of bobbing your head from side to side, up and down, trying to see over and round the screen to follow your line. Wrists swell with the work they have to perform on the wheel and the gear-changing. Legs cramp up, arms ache and your back develops an uncomfortably cold sweat. Despite ear-plugs and covers on the helmet you can't deaden the continuous howl of the engine and you finish nearly stone-deaf.

'Car races are usually longer than motor-bike races, so the mental exhaustion from unbroken concentration leaves you drained and desperately tired.

'The driver is jammed tight, legs straight out, with just about enough room to move his arms. If he moves them fractionally too far trying to relax them he usually cracks them on something, so he might as well not have bothered. Then, above all, there's the nagging fear that if you hit something hard you're sitting on what is virtually a petrol bomb, with fuel pipes all around you.

'After every race, Jackie Stewart goes to visit a physiotherapist to have the aches and pains of racing soothed away. Jackie's physiotherapist in Glasgow has taught him a series of relaxing exercises that he can perform while he is racing. They amount to hardly anything—just stretching his neck upwards and forcing his shoulders down as he's driving, but they've helped to ease the discomforts he used to suffer. They don't completely alleviate the pain—nothing could do that—but they have made its onset a little more gradual.

'Jim Clark once had to travel something like a hundred miles in a race so tired, and with his neck muscles so weakened, that he had to allow his head to flop on to the side screen for support. It was the only method he could use to keep going. Without that support his head would have lolled painfully from side to side until he was forced to stop. I can imagine how he felt, but he wouldn't give up.

'I remember driving in Sicily, on the circuit at Enna, where the road surface was in a diabolical condition. My face was gashed with flying stones in training. In the race I wound a bandage around the bare flesh that would have showed under the helmet—but the stones still got through. I had three lenses to my goggles, one over the other, and had to slip them off as each one became too scratched to see through. I spent the race driving half blind.

'A motor-bike offers far more comfort; it doesn't have the same confining features as a motor-car. On a bike you have far more freedom. You can sit upright, stretch your legs and have a look round. The works machines are tailor-made for the rider, the saddles are fitted at the most comfortable position. The footrests can be lifted or lowered to suit the individual rider's taste and length of leg.

'It's only occasionally, in races like the TT where the big events are run over 226 miles, that the rider feels any discomfort. The TT is particularly arduous; a test not only of the machine but of the man as well. If the weather is cold and wet you get cramp, and your fingers crook themselves arthritically into the shape of the grips. But at least you have room to move them, and to stretch your legs to fight off cramp.

'When the weather's been really bad on the island I've seen riders have to be lifted off their bikes. They've been bent almost double, backs arched, fingers drained of colour, like old men. But it doesn't happen at every race. In cars, discomfort is taken as part of the job.

'I think that to race a car you have to be really tough and resilient and most certainly as fit as any athlete. Of course you have to be fit to race bikes too, but they aren't nearly so demanding on your physical reserves.

'I don't very often suffer physically from bike racing; my body is attuned to it. It's developed my shoulders and forearms to the point where I feel little fatigue. My breathing is easy and relaxed and my arm- and stomach-muscles are really strong from the constant riding. I never do any exercises—riding keeps me fit. In between seasons I keep fit by skiing, water-skiing and playing golf and squash.

'Because I'm so attuned to the position I have to assume on a bike, and because, when the heat is off, I can sit up and stretch, I hardly ever feel any effects. What I do feel is the mental strain; the concentration has to be so deep, especially in vital races, that it's inevitable I should end a race feeling mentally washed out.

'It could be, I imagine, that motor-cycle racing comes more naturally to me than Formula One racing did, and because of this the mental strain is not nearly so severe. I finish bike races feeling a damn sight fresher than ever I did when I had finished a car race.

'Give me a bike every time.'

9. Three to Remember

What is Mike's most memorable race? What aspects of it, for what reasons, make it the one that stands alone, above all the others?

These are questions that could be fiercely argued, because a hundred people could have a hundred varying views, according to their particular ideas of excitement and of what constitutes a memorable race.

Mike, Stan Hailwood and I ran a poll between us on what we thought was the most memorable race. The answers we came up with illustrated in three entirely different views just what does make a race memorable. It showed us, too, that the view depends completely on one's own particular and specific interest.

While our opinions differed widely, we were remarkably unanimous on one point—the place. Out of all the classics run on the world's circuits the Isle of Man TT, once again, figured prominently.

I posed the question as we sat on the terrace of Mike's hotel in Douglas, the island's capital. The answers came back without hesitation. Mike replied, 'The 1963 Senior.' 'Rubbish,' said his father. 'Your best was the one you didn't win. The Junior of '65.' Then they both looked across at me for my answer, which was—and still is—the 1965 Senior, when Mike fell off, climbed back on and won.

It is worth examining each of these three races in detail; each one has its own outstanding merit.

The 1965 Senior, I would say, was an unforgettable race. It clearly demonstrated the full force of Mike's will to win, his courage and his determination never to give up while the engine is still turning over, however erratically. This, in my opinion, was his finest hour, the race in which he literally pulled himself off the floor to win in what is undoubtedly the most stirring TT performance of all time.

Towards the end of the third lap Mike was well ahead, with nothing to trouble his mind other than the normal worry about the machine's reliability and willingness to stay the course. The red MV was handling beautifully, the engine-note sweet and unfaltering.

Passing Sarah's Cottage, he pressed his chest more closely against the tank and tucked his chin behind the fly-spattered screen, hanging on tightly as the bike accelerated smoothly and quickly up the hill that forms the exit from the Cottage.

He couldn't see the oil slick filming a puddle in the middle of his line through the next section. Suddenly the heavy bike slipped sideways and keeled over beyond the point of no return. Mike and the MV parted company at around 80 m.p.h. Mike was thrown along the rain-sodden asphalt on his back. As he skidded and bounced, his arms flung protectively round his head, his race number, tightly stitched to the back of his leathers, was ripped clean off. The MV careered crazily behind him, battered almost out of recognition by the road. When man and machine came to rest, Mike found himself flat on his back . . . looking into the eyes of an amused Giacomo Agostini, who had fallen at the same spot a little earlier.

But if Agostini thought he was going to have his team-mate for company during the remainder of the race he was wrong.

Mike got gingerly to his feet and cautiously felt his limbs. He waved aside the helpful marshals who had run to his aid, and stared at the MV. The windscreen was cracked wide open and flapping loose. The fairing was scarred down its entire length. The trumpet-shaped megaphones were squashed almost flat. The gear lever was buckled, the handlebars bent out of line, and half a footrest had been sliced off.

He heaved the bike upright and propped it against a grassy verge, then set about putting as much right as he could. He kicked furiously at the handlebars until they were as near true as he could get them under the circumstances. He didn't know whether the engine had been seriously damaged by the beating it had suffered, but he wouldn't give up.

Against all race regulations, he turned the machine round so that it pointed back down the hill towards the oncoming traffic, and pushed for all he was worth. The marshals diplomatically looked the other way. The bike fired; it was still fighting fit. He swerved round in the road and set off towards the pits at the starting-point. The crowd, who knew Mike was overdue and had given him up, were startled to see an extremely second-hand-looking MV tearing past them, the knife-edge of the damaged screen swishing dangerously close to the rider's face.

When Mike steered the wounded machine into the pits the impact was devastating. Spectators crowded as close as they could to have a look and came away shaking their heads. The thousands of people in the stands groaned their disappointment.

The mechanics looked on in despair at the wreckage. But Mike, as casual as if he were sitting in an armchair, stayed astride the machine, resolutely refusing to quit. He insisted they did what they could, then helped to rip off the shattered windscreen.

There was nothing more they could do, and seventy seconds later he pushed himself back into the race. The spectators who had given up hope rose to their feet to cheer wildly as the familiar ear-splitting note of the MV announced Mike's intention.

Mike was faced with the agony of riding with no protection for his face at 160 m.p.h. The rain was needles on his face, water swilled into his goggles and beaded the outside until he was riding almost blindly round the most dangerous circuit in the world.

As if this wasn't enough to worry him, there was more trouble on its way. The engine began to act up, and on lap five he motored into the pits. We all thought that at last he had seen sense and pulled out—and who could have blamed him? It would have been a glorious retirement. *But he wanted to win.*

Sixty-seven seconds later he was on his way again. The mechanics had fixed a throttle-slide on one of the four cylinders, but as soon as he got going again the slide jammed wide open. For what was left of the race it refused to shut down. It ran on full bore and he had to keep his hand on the brake to hold the bike in check on the corners.

It needs a special brand of courage to ride to win under these circumstances, to ride hard into the corners with an engine that has gone haywire and is trying to take you faster than is safe. The record-books in years to come will show only that in 1965 S. M. B. Hailwood won the Senior at a speed of 91·69 m.p.h.—the slowest 500 cc win on the island since 1950. But what a story lies behind that simple, unrevealing result! To anybody who was there—and there were 100,000 people—the memory will last for ever.

Mike described it this way. 'I would say that the '65 Senior was just about my dodgiest ride ever. I was winding it on up the hill when suddenly I was on my backside, leading the bike by about five yards towards the start and finish. I couldn't believe I wasn't hurt. There wasn't a scratch on me, but the bike was in a hell of a mess. I thought I'd had it for the race. When I picked it up I shoved it the wrong way down the hill to get it started. If anybody had reported me to the organizers for breaking the regulations I'd have strangled him. I had only one thought—and that was to get going again. I didn't care how many laws I broke. I suppose I could have been robbed of the race if anybody had reported me.'

The fact is, everybody seemed to know that Mike had broken a rule, but it didn't get to the ears of the officials. Or did it?

It would have to have been an extremely brave official to snatch victory from Mike's grasp, and there were certainly no complaints from any of the riders who might have seen him. A marshal did take pictures of the offence—but he kept them hidden away for weeks.

Mike added, 'The main worry I had was when I got back to the pits after the spill. I wondered if the scrutineers would allow me to carry on. They gave the bike a hard look, but they said it would be okay to continue.

'You can't imagine what it's like, riding without a screen. I put a strip of red tape over my nose, but there was nothing I could do to protect the rest of my face. It felt as if my cheeks were tearing away from the corners of my mouth. I was almost stone-deaf from the rush of the wind.'

'Didn't it occur to you to pack it up?' I asked him.

'What for?' he said. 'The bike was still running, and I had a fair chance of winning. I never even thought about the effects of the crash. I dismissed it from my mind as soon as I found I was still in one piece. As I said, winning is too important to give up that easily.'

To my mind this was Mike's finest success. It was, I think, the complete answer to all those critics who had given more credit to the machine than to the man. His skill, in my opinion, could not be questioned. His bravery had had little opportunity to show itself in such an obvious way and when it did get the chance he never hesitated for a moment.

The 1965 Junior was one race that Mike didn't win, but it's still the one which gets Stan Hailwood's preference as his son's finest performance.

Mike described it like this. 'The 350 three-cylinder MV I had was a new machine, and virtually untried. I rode it for a few laps in practice for the West German Grand Prix at the Nürburgring, but it quit on me.

'I still wasn't too happy about it when we arrived on the island. It was handling very badly, and the mechanics had to work hard trying to sort it out. On the last practice session for the Junior the weather was terrible, pouring with rain, and I couldn't give it the sort of run through I would have liked.

'The MV boys stayed up all night trying to patch it up from odd bits off the 500. They switched the forks and doctored the shockers. We had to ask for an extension until 9 p.m. to put off the official scrutineering, but the bike still wasn't really in good order. Worse, it was a completely unknown quantity. I had no idea how it would behave in the race, but there was nothing more we could do. I was stuck with it and I knew I would just have to make the best of it.

'Stan and I discussed tactics over breakfast on the morning of the race. We tried to work out the best way to beat Jim Redman's Honda; but in the end I decided it was useless, a waste of time, and the best plan would be to go as fast as possible and hope for a break.

'Jim was seeded to start thirty seconds ahead of me. I watched him from the start and he got off to a flying opening. My bike was sluggish away from the flag and I lost a second or so on the start.'

Nobody gave Mike a chance against the superior Honda piloted by Jim Redman, who was on peak form. The race was scheduled to be a Honda demonstration run. Interest in it as a competition was very limited even before the start, but within a few minutes excitement was flooding back. The course commentators, frantically totting up their times, revealed that Mike was catching Redman, narrowing the margin at every section of the circuit, riding with furious determination.

Stan Hailwood, recalling the race, said with pride, 'By the end of the first lap Mike had taken nineteen seconds from Jim's lead and shattered the lap record from a standing start by clocking 102·85 miles an hour. I'd have given anything to watch Mike throwing that MV about trying to catch Jim. It must have been a wonderful treat to watch him going through the tricky bits, particularly the extremely difficult parts from the Mountain Box down to the start.

'It wasn't difficult to realize that he was at full stretch; to break the lap record from a standing start was proof enough of that. Many people have since come over to me and said that he was in absolutely superb form, apparently throwing all caution to the winds in his efforts to master the strangeness of the MV and to outpace Jim's Honda.'

Mike finished the first lap only fractionally behind Jim, but forged ahead on the second and third laps. His determination over-shadowed his lack of confidence in the MV. It was a startling reversal. By the end of lap three he had opened up an incredible lead of fifteen seconds.

Mike and Jim Redman both came into the pits at the close of the third lap. The tension had the spectators biting their nails. They stopped thirty yards from each other; now every second was precious. Redman's mechanic, who had been crouching like a sprinter, sprang to the side of the Honda as it rolled to a dead-straight, perfectly executed halt. Jim flipped open the filler cap as he braked. Just behind him, at the same instant, Mike steered the MV under the point of the petrol nozzle held by a mechanic. But he was obviously having trouble with the machine. The crowd jammed shoulder to shoulder in the grandstand leapt to their feet; but they hardly knew which way to look —to Redman in pit No. 7, or to Mike in No. 14.

Jim glanced anxiously back over his shoulder as he mentally counted to nineteen seconds, the time he had allowed for a nineteen-litre fill-up. He saw Mike's mechanic struggling desperately with the MV's rear-end. He didn't waste any time getting away again, and roared off, leaving Mike stranded and helpless at the pits.

Mike explained the trouble. 'There was an oil leak somewhere that was bleeding the life out of the bike. We couldn't find it. There was oil all over the back wheel and we had to towel it off, but we still couldn't trace the source of the leak. We tightened as many nuts as we could lay spanners on, but it didn't make any difference. The oil still seeped out. The chain had stretched four inches and was so slack that it kept jumping off the sprocket, and I had spent all of lap three leaping and hopping along the road like a kangaroo.

'We found out later that the oil leak was coming not from the engine but from a chain-oiler. The bike didn't last long before the chain finally snapped.'

In fact it snapped only thirteen miles after Mike had re-started his attempt to wrest back the lead from Redman.

'When Jim looked over his shoulder towards me in the pits,' added Mike, 'I almost shouted to him that the race was his, but he wouldn't have believed me.'

Stan Hailwood said, 'I was an extremely proud father that day. Mike had shown that he could certainly ride with the best of them over the TT course.

'From the beginning nobody gave him a chance, yet he almost pulled off a great win against all the odds—and they were stacked high against him. The machine was far from perfect, and it's a miracle that he got round as well as he did.

'I've often wondered what the eventual outcome would have been if all the gremlins had been ironed out of the MV. If Mike had been able to race the bike a couple of times before the TT it would undoubtedly have been put right in time for the Junior.

'If, for instance, Count Agusta had allowed him to ride it at the Italian Grand Prix the previous September, Mike would have discovered that the chain was a type not suited to the job it would have to contend with on the island. Instead of permitting Mike to give it an airing the Count turned us down, much to our annoyance. His lack of foresight lost Mike the Junior.

'Even though Mike failed to finish the '65 Junior the race was none the less memorable, and, I am sure, his finest showing. It had everything. He refused steadfastly to accept that he was a beaten man and was prepared to take chances to prove it; it was a fine example to other riders. It taught them that the underdog can still bite.'

Mike had listened to the two views on his finest race with little comment other than that demanded of him as further explanation. He expressed the view that to his mind neither one could be regarded as *the* race. . . .

'*The 1963 Senior* was the best for me; and it happened in what, to my mind, was the most satisfying season of my career. The other two races mentioned were probably dramatic and exciting for the spectators, but the '63 Senior gave me the greatest personal satisfaction.

'That was the year that Geoff Duke persuaded Gileras to make a comeback to racing. Contrary to what many people thought at the time, I welcomed the competition; after all the hoo-ha about my winning "because there was nobody or nothing competitive enough" it was a good opportunity for me to show them how wrong they were.

'I had a good season throughout 1963. I was riding well within myself, without stretching myself too far; I didn't seem to be taking any risks. I was full of confidence and it made me feel good.

'This was the mood I was in when I got to the island for the TT. The fact that John Hartle and Phil Read had been signed by Geoff Duke and were going to ride the Gileras against me didn't worry me too much. I was looking forward to a really demanding dice. I wasn't the only one, because the influx of visitors to the island reached record levels. The motor-cycle writers were forecasting lap times of around 106 m.p.h. in what was going to be a much tighter race than for years previously.

'I knew that if the three of us could keep going the race was certainly going to be a quick one, but I hesitated to make any rash comments on the likely speed. I knew, too, that the main danger would come from

John Hartle; he was well used to riding multi-cylinder machinery and I don't think anybody knows the island better than he does.

'In my list of the best riders in the business, Hartle would certainly be in the top three; he's among the best I've seen during my lifetime. He, I decided, was the man I would have to watch. Read wasn't quite so experienced, and I had no serious worries in that department.

'When the ballot was made to seed the positions for the start I was delighted to discover that I had been allotted a place ten seconds behind John. That's a tremendous psychological spur, because you know that once you get the man in sight you only have to stay with him to win. The onus is on him to force the pace, to stay ahead and try to work out a speed that will maintain the margin. He's got to go hell for leather, then, having done that, has to see if the effort has been good enough to keep him on that ten-second mark. More important, he has to try to build up a lead with nobody to chase, no target to aim for. Whereas in this case, so far as I was concerned, I did have somebody to chase. I knew I had only to go hard enough to catch him and I'd swept away his advantage. After that it becomes a matter of nursing the engine and watching the target trying his damnedest to shake you off.

'John shot away from the start as if the devil was after him, and he'd clearly been foxing in practice because his speed in the race was much better than it had been in training. He was really trying, because he worked himself into a glorious slide at Quarter Bridge then set his wheels into the gutter at Cronk-ny-Mona. He was pulling out all the stops, and I knew I would have a hell of a job to beat him.

'There was only one tactic to employ and that was to go as quickly as I could. It paid off, and on the Sulby Straight, about three-quarters of the way round on the first lap, I got to within a hundred yards of him. I'd managed, somehow, to clip back the ten seconds, and I had him in my sights. John rode furiously but I didn't dare let myself be shaken off. I had to stay with him. I knew that I couldn't relax for a moment, but I knew he was in the same boat.

'I stayed tucked in his slipstream for a while, then made up my mind to get away. I thought that if I did run into any trouble I'd better have some time in hand to sort it out. As it happened it was a wise move. On the third lap the gear spring-return went bust; it was working only intermittently. I had to keep leaning out of the saddle like some fancy rodeo rider to hook the gears in by hand.

'It would go down two gears then stop. It wasn't too dangerous provided I slowed down enough before going into the corners. I had to give myself time to duck down, yank the gear lever back into the right cog, get up again, ride round the corner and then pull another gear in.

'It was a bit rocky once or twice, but when I got the hang of it there wasn't too much of a problem. I knew I'd built up a fair lead, and provided the trouble didn't worsen I could cope with it all right.

'I'd have never put it right if I'd stopped—everything that had gone wrong was inside the box. There was no point in signalling the pits either, they couldn't do anything to help. I don't believe in giving away too much, and it might have given a hint to John. As it was, he had no idea I was having trouble.

'I knew he was just waiting to take over and I had to keep going as hard as I knew how. Under the circumstances I don't think I did such a bad job....'

That understatement might suggest that Mike just managed to scrape home at an unspectacular pace. Perhaps the reason is that he had no idea quite how fast he had circuited those gruelling 37¾ miles. It is worth re-recording in the light of the setbacks he suffered.

His first lap was a flyer which broke the record from a standing start. He was clocked at a staggering 106·30 m.p.h. Despite the trouble he lapped at nothing less than 104 m.p.h. for the remaining five laps and, in the second lap, was timed at 106·31 m.p.h.

I remember telling Mike after the race what his times were. He stood unbelieving in the winner's enclosure and said, 'You're joking. Let's have a look at that score-board.' His eye swept the times painted in white down the length of the board. 'Well, I never. I can hardly believe it,' he said. 'I was just tootling round once I'd caught up with John. I didn't seem to be racing at all. It was more like a fast tour. I felt as fit at the finish as I did when I started; I could have gone on for another six laps.'

Why was that Mike's best race? He explained, 'I suppose because I had something to race against. Let's face it, Hartle is no slouch, he lapped at more than 105 m.p.h. three times. Read wasn't so much of a threat, but he wasn't hanging about either.

'I felt that I had won against some real opposition. The Gileras, as their times showed, were certainly well on form, even if they had been laid off for six years. It was a strong challenge, and I was happy that I had the ability to fight it off. That's what made it all so satisfying.

'When I found that I had broken the record, without, to my mind, really trying, I felt even more stimulated. The other two races you mentioned were satisfying in their own ways, for completely different reasons. This one gave me the greatest kick. It's the one I'll always remember as my best. After all, it was a genuine race in the fullest sense of the word. At least it started out that way.

'And that was to have been my last TT. I was so keen at that time to switch over to motor racing that I was going to quit motor-cycles. The bitter experience I had in Grand-Prix cars made me change my mind back again. Though, even if I had made the switch, I'm not so sure that I wouldn't have taken a fortnight off to have a go at the TT. It gets in your blood: there's not a race like it, anywhere in the world.'